HOW IT ALL BEGAN

HOW IT ALL BEGAN

The Stories Behind Those Famous Names

MAURICE BAREN

First published in 1992 by
Smith Settle Ltd
Ilkley Road
Otley   West Yorkshire   LS21 3JP

ISBN 1 870071 92 1

British Library
Cataloguing-in-Publication Data:
A catalogue record for this book
is available from the British Library

Printed and bound by
SMITH SETTLE
Ilkley Road
Otley   West Yorkshire   LS21 3JP

Dedication

To my loving wife Judith
and to our children
Andrew, Peter and Caroline
for their patience with all the paper,
for their encouragement and love.

My sincere thanks.

Acknowledgments

The registered trade marks, logos and trade names in this book have been reproduced with the kind permission of the companies concerned. They are all strictly copyright, and must not be reproduced without the companies' express permission. Thanks are due to the undermentioned companies and individuals for permission to reproduce the illustrations and logos listed below:

Addis Ltd, pp118–119; Allinson, p3; Anchor Foods Ltd, p5; Avon Products Inc, p7; Baxters, pp10–11; Birds Eye Wall's Ltd, p16, 114–115; Bissell Inc, USA, p17; Britains Ltd, p20; Brooke Bond Oxo, pp21–22; Cadbury, pp23–25; Cadbury Schweppes, pp93–95; C & J Clark Ltd, pp26–27; Coca-Cola Great Britain, p28; Colman's of Norwich, pp29–30; Corning Ltd, p85; CPC (UK) Ltd, p4, 18–19, 71; Damart, p31; John Dickinson, p32; Dunlop Slazenger International Ltd, p97; Ercol Furniture Ltd, p34; Elida Gibbs Ltd, p38, 81–82; Fyffes Group Ltd, p35; General Foods, pp14–15; The Gillette Company, pp39–41; Goblin Ltd, pp42–43; Gossard, pp44–45;

R Griggs & Co Ltd, p33; H J Heinz Co Ltd, pp46–48; Hestair Maclaren Ltd, p70; Hoover Ltd, p49; Humbrol Ltd, p2; The Jacobs Bakery Ltd, pp56–57; Jacobs Suchard Tobler, p110; Johnson & Johnson Ltd, p58; Johnson's Wax Polish, p59; Kellogg Company, pp60–61; Kodak, pp62–63; Ladybird Books Ltd, pp64–65; Lego UK Ltd, pp66–67; Lever Bros Ltd, pp68–69; Lyle & Scott, p123; Mars Confectionery, p72; Max Factor, p73; McVitie's Group, p74; Moulinex Swan Ltd, p107; Societe des Products Nestlé SA, pp88–89; Omega Ltd, p77; Parker Pen UK Ltd, pp79–80; Peter Pan Playthings Ltd, p83; J B Pettigrew, p100; Pretty Polly Ltd, p84; Procter & Gamble Ltd, p113; Raleigh Industries Ltd,

p86; Rank Hovis Ltd, pp52–53; RHM Foods Ltd, p6; James Robertson & Sons, p87; Scholl Consumer Products Ltd, pp90–91; Silver Cross Ltd, p96; Smiths Food Group, p100; SmithKline Beecham, pp12–13, 50–51; Smith & Nephew Medical Ltd, p101; Staedtler (UK) Ltd, pp102–103; Stanley Gibbons Ltd, pp36–37; Start-rite Shoes Ltd, pp104–105; Tate & Lyle PLC, p108; Thermos Ltd, p109; 3M, p92; Tom Smith Group Ltd, pp98–99; Trebor Bassett Ltd, pp8–9; Tupperware, p111; R Twining & Co Ltd, p112; Unilever, p16, 68–69, 114; John Waddington PLC, pp75–76, 106; Wander Ltd, p78; Waterman Pens (UK) Ltd, p116; Winsor & Newton, p117; The Wrigley Co Ltd, pp120–121; Yale Security Products Ltd, p122.

Information from *The Gillette Company 1901–1976* is quoted with the permission of The Gillette Company.

Additional illustrations were provided by the author.

Contents

Author's Note

I would like to thank a large number of people who have helped in many ways to enable this book to come together. The sources of material have been very varied. Some small helpful clue has often led me on a wider search to find even more material. I am therefore most grateful to those who have loaned material, not least all the companies represented within the book, but also those who have encouraged me, checked material and given words of wisdom. I would particularly mention Dr Fred Kidd, Peggy and Tom Hewitt, Geoffrey Greenwood, Tony and Jacquie Jones, Duncan Clark, David Hanks, Ian Grimshaw, David Binns, Harold Baker, Coralie Stocks, Peter Longbottom, Lucia Ercolani, Mrs M R Steel, Mr J E Bewley, Victor Laycock, Kay Randall, Victor H Watson CBE, Mr I F Wayman, John Barrett, Miss V Warren, Mr J B Pettigrew, Peter H Kimpton, Donald Raine and Anne Arana.

I have tried to ensure that full acknowledgement has been given of others' material, but if anything has been wrongly attributed or if any person feels I have failed to give them credit, I do apologise. Over many, many years of collecting it is often very difficult to always remember from where a little bit of paper came!

Introduction

It was in 1882 that Henry Heinz said 'Our market is the world'. Since that time – and indeed before then – many other potential businessmen and women have had similar thoughts: an idea has been born, they have nurtured it, given it their all and seen it develop. But in how many cases do we take for granted their inspiration and work? Indeed, in some cases we do not even know their name.

This book seeks to reveal some of the stories behind the people and their products, perhaps to give answers to questions that previously have had to remain unanswered. Unfortunately, stories such as these are continually being lost for all time as companies go out of business or are swallowed up by large conglomerates, and archive material is either dispersed or destroyed.

Henry Heinz was prepared to do anything 'to earn an honest cent', but it was the sales of his garden products which started him on his way to success. A call on Fortnum and Mason in London gave him the break from being an American company to becoming a worldwide company. His beliefs in pure food and high Christian principles led him to produce goods and have business ethics of the highest standards.

Also in America, King Camp Gillette came from a family of inventors, and his desire to become an inventor became an uncontrollable craving. He met William Painter, the inventor of the crown cork, who told him to invent something which would sell over and over again – we know the result, but there was much hard work and desperation in between.

Yet another American, George Eastman, saw in early photography an opportunity to develop new equipment and techniques which would revolutionise the taking of 'snaps'.

Two of these gave their name to their product, the third invented a new word, Kodak, a name that has also become known worldwide.

In Britain, Tom Smith developed the first Christmas cracker, taking and developing a French idea, but adding to it his own original thought, which came as he looked at the Yule log burning in the grate. The ill-health of some other person has inspired people to create remedies or alternative products which might improve the sick person's quality of life. Alfred Bird was one such person – his wife had stomach problems and could not eat eggs or yeast-based products. As a result of Alfred Bird's skills, in what today we would call food technology, we now have 'Custard Powder' and 'Baking Powder', and she had her favourite custard!

This book contains many previously unpublished facts and illustrations about those things which we wear, eat or drink, or which have changed our everyday life. It is a dipping book, a gift book, an encyclopaedia of social history – a book to have on the shelf, ready to look up those facts which previously have been so difficult to trace.

For those at school it will be a ready reference book for project work. For those studying economics or marketing it will give an insight into how others have found success. To staff in museums it will provide leads into stories which can result in interesting displays. To all it is a book which will give new insights into how and why products have been developed, and how they have often become generic names.

Maurice Baren
1992

In 1939, Nicholas Kove formed a company to manufacture rubber toys filled with air. He had a fondness for words ending in 'ix', and he also believed that every good company should have a name which would bring it to the head of any trade catalogue listing. He hit upon the idea of the name 'Airfix' which aptly covered both these points, whilst at the same time representing the type of product he was manufacturing.

During the company's formative years it expanded considerably, but in the war years, due to shortage of materials, it had to diversify and included in its new products were combs – in 1947 it was claimed to be the largest manufacturer of combs in England. However the war years, and Mr Kove's ill-health, caused a recession in the company and so after the war he strove to rebuild his company by returning to the manufacture of children's toys.

Shortly after this, John Gray and Ralph Ehrmann joined the company and they saw the potential of injection-moulded construction kits. In 1952 the first injection-moulded construction kit – of Sir Francis Drake's ship the *Golden Hind* – was launched. They were made of the then new plastic material known as polystyrene OS, which included a rubber type of compound.

The models were submitted to F W Woolworth. Woolworths gave them an order so large that it took nine months to complete, moulding both day and night. It was then that they fully realised the economic potential of accurate model construction kits and turned their attention to aircraft, in 1953 producing the Airfix Spitfire model. This was marketed exclusively through Woolworths and has continued to be a best seller.

From 1953 to 1957 the company produced more construction kits, covering sections such as aircraft, historical ships, veteran cars, trackside accessories, 00 figures and historical subjects. Each kit produced was accurately scaled down, a necessary feature, as they now were bought by enthusiasts as well as children.

In 1957 the company went public, and shortly after this Mr Kove died. Later the company made a wider entry into the toy market and among its popular ranges were the well-known Weebles – the wobbly men, women and children. In 1971 they added to their subsidiaries the famous Meccano Dinky Company, to be followed later by the Triang Pedigree range of toys.

Airfix's current model of the Golden Hind

Thomas Richard Allinson was born at Grange-over-Sands on the edge of the Lake District in 1858. He left home when he was fifteen years old to become a chemist's assistant. With the money he saved, and with some help from his stepfather, he went to Edinburgh University to study medicine, qualifying as a doctor when he was twenty-three years old.

He was keenly interested in diet and how it affected people's health. He was already an advocate of wholemeal bread and had become a vegetarian, recommending natural cures for the treatment of illness.

In 1886 he wrote his first book – *A System of Hygienic Medicine* – which expounded his theories on diet and exercise as a way to good health. He was later to write other books on lung complaints, stomach diseases, rheumatism, vegetarian cookery and, not least, a book entitled *The Advantages of Wholemeal Bread*. At that time, white bread was the vogue and virtually no mills were producing flour to his standard.

In 1888, Dr Allinson set up his own practice in London and in 1892 he acquired a small mill called Cyclone Mills in Bethnal Green. He formed the Natural Food Company, coining the slogan 'Health without Medicine'.

Allinson promoted his beliefs in print

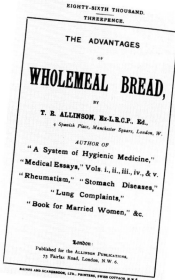

He sold his flour to bakers, providing them with certificates which stated that they were making wholemeal bread to his standard, with flour from his mill. Where patients did not have a bakery nearby, he encouraged them to make their own bread with his flour.

In 1921 the company acquired the lease to Queens Mill, Castleford, Yorkshire, and one in Newport, Monmouthshire. To centralise the milling of the stoneground whole-wheat flour, the company decided to enlarge the Castleford mill in 1979–80, making it the largest stonegrinding flour mill in the world, with eighteen pairs of stones.

Today the Castleford mill produces the 100% stoneground flour to the same high standards that Dr Tom Allinson stood for. The Allinson name is also licensed to various companies, such as Allied Bakeries who produce wrapped bread – 'wi' nowt taken out'.

Ambrosia

TM Reg'd.

In 1915, Alfred Morris was on board a ship to France, when he met a Mr Hatmaker, an American who was trying to interest investors in his patent machines which were already in use in France.

Whilst Alfred already had a leather business in London, he was neverthe-less interested in the methods used and met Mr Hatmaker, as arranged, in Paris a few days later. Alfred was sorry to find his new friend depressed because of the lack of interest in his dried milk proposals. Alfred, being a shrewd businessman and seeing the opportunity of setting up a potentially profitable business, suggested he should find somewhere in England to set up the drying machines. On his return to England he went to see Lloyd George with a sample of the dried milk from France, asking if it would help the Government's food policy for the war effort. He was told

An early tin

that it would if he could produce full cream milk.

Alfred Morris' hobby was fishing – and he thought weather conditions which gave good fishing would also give good supplies of milk. He decided on Lifton in Devon, where he gained the support of the landlord of a local inn. He helped set up a meeting with local farmers, and they agreed to supply fifty gallons of milk a day.

The creamery at Lifton went into production in 1917, the milk being delivered by horse and cart. A sample of the full cream dried milk was sent to the War Office, and, after testing, they gave Ambrosia an order for 300 tons. The Ambrosia Creamery started up with less than a dozen staff and a Model T Ford for collecting the milk. Special trains were also laid on from Launceston to Lifton to bring in the factory staff, the line running straight up to the factory.

Ambrosia, in the dictionary, is the food drink of the immortals, the elixir of life, and something divinely sweet to taste or smell. Being a small company, they could not afford advertising and the sales were through the welfare centres for infant feeding. A useful means of advertising came about when Ambrosia Dried Milk was introduced

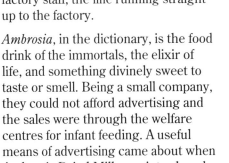

Ambrosia CREAMED RICE *Milk Pudding*

SERVE ALONE OR WITH FRUIT OR JAM – IT'S DELICIOUS!

to James Pascall Ltd, who were so impressed with it that they would use no other in their chocolate. An arrangement was made for the use of the Ambrosia trade mark and Ambrosia chocolate became well known.

A significant development in Lifton in 1933 was the introduction of tinned cream – it was the only tinned Devon cream on the market.

The introduction of their famous rice pudding followed from an idea by Metal Box, who supplied them with their tins. Metal Box had a formula for a canned rice pudding, but it involved making and cooking the pudding before canning, which was not very good. They exper-imented with filling the tin with the rice first, then using the Devon cream and putting in the full cream milk and sugar separately after heat treatment and homogenisation, and allowing the rice pudding to cook in the can. In 1937, Ambrosia was the first company to market rice pudding in a can, under the brand name Ambrosia Creamed Rice. During the war the Red Cross included tins of the creamed rice in prisoner-of-war parcels, and after the war the company received many letter of thanks from ex-prisoners.

Henry Reynolds, a Cornishman, emigrated to New Zealand, taking up dairy farming in an area known as Waikato. He built its first butter factory and on the morning of the 3rd November 1886 he made the first churning. He chose 'Anchor' as a brand name – why we do not know. However we do know that for an early settler, its symbolism for reliability and safe arrival would be important. Its image was easily identified, and would transfer neatly onto the surface of the butter.

At the Melbourne Exhibition in 1886, Anchor butter was awarded first prize and this encouraged Henry to extend his business. Ten years later he sold his company, and the brand name, to the New Zealand Dairy Association; in succeeding years, other amalgamations took place and

The first Anchor butter pack from 1924

eventually the New Zealand Dairy Company was formed.

Before the Second World War, most housewives bought their butter from a large block displayed on the grocer's counter, it being packed in individual amounts in front of them. In 1924, however, Anchor had started pre-packing their butter to encourage customers to choose their brand. These pats were produced at a packing factory in Upper Thames Street in London.

By 1969, Anchor was the biggest selling butter brand in Britain.

When Britain became a member of the EEC, New Zealand's exports were restricted, but still they managed to retain their position as the leading brand in this country, and today they have the world's most advanced butter and cheese packing plant at Swindon.

A 1935 shop display card

For you

from the fresh, green pasturelands of sunny New Zealand

The most delightful butter you can possibly get. Butter you can be proud of on all occasions. A pure, skilfully made product of finest cream, rich in *natural* vitamins, golden with sunshine. There's nothing like it for growing children, and for people of all ages, its wonderful nutritive qualities have been the subject of high tribute by eminent doctors. New Zealand sends you the best of all butter at a price within the reach of everyone. Look for it at your grocer's. Buy it regularly.

NEW ZEALAND BUTTER

ATORA

In a college in Paris, towards the end of the nineteenth century, some of Gabriel Hugon's friends filled his chemistry beaker with liquid fat as a prank. It solidified. Several years later he remembered this schoolboy joke when he watched his wife chop suet from a joint of beef. The incident was the start of a business.

Gabriel had, by now, set up an engraving business in Manchester, but in 1893 he founded a suet-making firm under the name of Atora. It is felt that the name was derived from *toro*, which is Spanish for bull. This is obviously linked to the fact that suet is the fat around the kidneys, in this case cows' kidneys as beef suet is the purest form, and this suet is shredded. Up to the early 1940s, Atora suet was delivered to shops in colourful wagons pulled by six pairs of Hereford bullocks. Later the same wagons joined the famous Chipperfields Circus.

Atora has a good storage life, proved by the fact that among the company's possessions is a tin which was taken by Captain Scott on his historic Antarctic trek in the early 1900s. It was returned to the company and the suet contents were still pure and intact.

Today Atora sells more than 2,500 tons of suet in Britain each year – enough to make 500,000 dumplings each day!

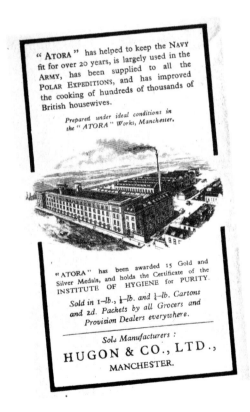

"ATORA" has helped to keep the NAVY fit for over 20 years, is largely used in the ARMY, has been supplied to all the POLAR EXPEDITIONS, and has improved the cooking of hundreds of thousands of British housewives.

Prepared under ideal conditions in the "ATORA" Works, Manchester.

"ATORA" has been awarded 15 Gold and Silver Medals, and holds the Certificate of the INSTITUTE OF HYGIENE for PURITY.

Sold in 1-lb., ½-lb. and ¼-lb. Cartons and 2d. Packets by all Grocers and Provision Dealers everywhere.

Sole Manufacturers :

HUGON & CO., LTD.,
MANCHESTER.

1932 EDITION

THE RECIPE BOOK OF "ATORA" The Good BEEF SUET

Avon

David H McConnell was an enterprising young American, who sold books on a door-to-door basis. To encourage business he gave away small phials of cologne. He soon discovered that his fragrances were in greater demand than his books, and in 1886 this gave him an idea of a new concept in the selling of beauty aids.

In a small room in Manhattan he started to manufacture a modest range of fragrances, and so the California Perfume Company was born. David McConnell had learnt that the best way of selling goods was direct to people's homes, and so he appointed ladies to sell his fragrances in the same highly personalised way. He also gave a pledge to all his customers – if a product was not satisfactory, their money would be refunded, a most unusual policy in those early days.

Within a decade the California Perfume Company had outgrown its small accommodation in Manhattan, and a new plant was built at Suffern, New York. Early in the 1930s a significant change took place. At the time the name 'Avon' was used for various products in the California Perfume Company's range. (Legend has it that Suffern's rolling hills and green valleys reminded Mr McConnell of the verdant Shakespearean countryside through which the River Avon flows.) In 1939 the growing cosmetics company became Avon Products Inc, 'Avon' also being chosen for its easy pronunciation, shortness and appeal.

At present over 1,600,000 representatives in more than 100 countries sell a range of over 700 products, and there are Avon subsidiaries in 30 countries spread over 5 continents.

The founder of the California Perfume Company – David H McConnell

Bassett's

Since before the time of Christ, people have enjoyed the taste of liquorice. Roman legionaries were issued with liquorice root to chew on their long marches. In this country, Chaucer tells us how one of his characters in the *Canterbury Tales* 'cheweth licorys to smellen swete'.

Around 1769 a Pontefract chemist produced the first 'Pomfret Cake' by adding other ingredients to the liquorice. Confectioners made the liquorice sweets into other shapes, many of which we are familiar with today – catherine wheels, bootlaces, pipes, etc.

George Bassett, the founder of the present company, was born in 1818 at Ashover near Chesterfield. When George was fourteen years old he commenced a seven year apprenticeship with a confectioner and fruiterer. Ten years later he was himself a 'Wholesale Confectioner, Lozenge Maker and British Wine Dealer'.

In 1851 he employed an apprentice, S M Johnson, who eventually became

George Bassett

the sole proprietor of the company in 1893, a link which was to be maintained until 1974.

The story goes that, in 1899, Charlie Thompson, a 'Bassett Traveller', was selling his products to a wholesaler in Leicester. During the course of his 'presentation' he accidentally knocked over his individual sample boxes onto the counter, spilling the sweets. The wholesaler, Mr Walker, had not been much impressed with the individual selections but liked the look of the 'mix' – Liquorice Allsorts had been born!

In 1884, W R Wilkinson founded his confectionery manufacturing business in a malt kiln in Southgate, Pontefract. As these premises became too small, a new factory was built in Skinner Lane, and named Britannia Works. In these early years a twenty year old lad called Walter Marshall came up from Somerset to Yorkshire to seek his fortune, and his family have been associated with the management of the company ever since.

After the First World War, Walter Marshall developed a new factory on the site of what had been a liquorice garden – today it is one of only two liquorice confectionery factories in the town, and the largest.

The Marshall family sold the much-respected business of Wilkinsons to the Sheffield-based Bassetts in 1961.

In 1926, Bassetts had gone public, and decided to look for a trademark which consumers would associate specifically with their company. The assignment was given to an advertising agency called Greenlys.

At that time the Michelin Man, a figure made from tyres and used to advertise the Michelin company's products, was proving to be very popular. The managing director of Greenlys, Mr Bull, suggested that something similar should be used to promote Bassetts' goods. It was decided to create a character called 'Bertie Bassett', who would be made entirely from units of confectionery.

Over the years, Bertie's appearance has changed quite considerably, and he has acquired a walking stick. In recent years he has also been given a face – this is because he now appears in television advertisements and it was decided that he should be seen to talk.

Sixty years on and Bertie is still a favourite – as are Liquorice Allsorts – with the public in this country, and in other lands ranging from Australia to Canada and the United States to name but a few. Similarly the range of products has now diversified to include not only liquorice sweets and novelties but also wine gums, chewing gums, medicated pastilles and lozenges.

A 1954 advert (above) *shows how
Bertie has changed* (right)

Baxters

In the gardens of large estates, gardeners were taught that a standard of excellence was important. This lesson was to become very important to George Baxter in his later life. He was one of fifty gardeners employed by the Duke of Richmond and Gordon, on the estate at Castle Gordon, midway between Aberdeen and Inverness.

His wife, Margaret, was an excellent cook, and particularly good at making jams and jellies from the luscious berries for which the area was, and still is, famous. In 1868, George gave up gardening, and opened a grocery shop in Spey Street, Fochabers. Margaret made her jams and jellies in the back of the shop, and soon sales were very good. Visitors to the area and members of shooting and fishing parties, especially the duke's guests, bought her specialities and ate them with great enthusiasm. So much did they enjoy them that they wrote from

George and Margaret Baxter

their homes and ordered further supplies – this was the start of the spread of the business into other parts of the country.

George and Margaret's son, William, grew up with a great love of the business and at an early age showed considerable ability as a salesman. He travelled by train to distant corners of Scotland and then returned by cycle, on his way selling goods and collecting orders for his parents' business. As a result of his abilities, and of course also the fine quality of the product he was selling, sales were such that it was necessary to construct a new jam factory in 1914.

William's wife, Ethel, was a force in the creation of this factory, and one Sunday the seventh duke, along with William and Ethel, visited the proposed site by the River Spey. Together they marked out the space and soon building was in progress. Since those days the factory has been extended many times, but it is still located on the same site by the river.

Over the years, William and Ethel realised that their part of Scotland, with its ready supply of venison, beef, game, fish, fruit and vegetables, was an ideal base for such a venture. They therefore started to also develop new and exciting recipes using these superb ingredients. She experimented with new ways of preserving the fresh flavour so that her delicacies could be fully enjoyed wherever they went. Some of the new recipes included jugged hare and now world famous Royal Game soup.

In the 1920s, having seen the business firmly established in Scotland, William felt the time had come for another extension – this time south. With letters of introduction from the duke, he travelled to London and went to both Harrods, and Fortnum and Mason. The journey was a real success and many orders returned to Fochabers. After the Second World War the rebuilding of the business was put into the hands of Gordon and Ian, the sons of William and Ethel.

Gordon's wife Ena was an artist but her new form of artistry was to change – soon she was to become an artist in food. Her art studio was to be replaced by the kitchen of her new home. Whilst looking at an American magazine, a recipe for Louisiana chicken gumbo soup caught her eye. A vital ingredient was okra, a green pepper, not available in Fochabers. Ena persevered, and substituted green beans from her own kitchen garden for the okra. That evening she tried it out on her husband, who said it should be canned immediately! Before that was to happen, Ena insisted that she

The original Royal Game soup

perfect it. Several new products arrived in this way. This was an exciting new period in the history of Baxters – it brought forth such varieties as Cock-a-Leekie, Poacher's Broth and of course the link from pre-war days, Royal Game soup.

From those humble beginnings has grown a major company employing some 600 workers, whose range of products increases year by year. New recipes include Lobster Bisque, Artichoke and Scallop soup, cranberry sauce, pickles, canned game birds and a wide range of traditional Scottish foodstuffs. Today, by all forms of transport, products reach sixty different countries throughout the world.

The 'Old Shop' in Fochabers

Beecham

Thomas Beecham was born in the Oxfordshire village of Curbridge in 1820. Although Thomas was a natural scholar and quick to learn, he had to leave school and join his father in the fields, working seven days each week.

By the age of twenty he went to live with his uncle at Kidlington, six miles from Oxford. It was there he began to roll and powder pills. The pills were made by hand in three basic stages. Certain substances were mixed by pestle and mortar, liquid ingredients were added, including water, until a stiff pliable mass formed, which was converted into pills by rolling on a marble slab and cutting it into strips. The pills would then be dusted with french chalk to prevent them sticking. They were finally shaped by rolling. Having been left to dry for several weeks, a coating would be applied. However, Thomas did not stay long in Kidlington, leaving to become an itinerant pedlar of pills.

To achieve his desire to be a vendor of medicines he moved to Wallgate in Wigan. Beecham settled near the market place, and began to sell his herbal remedy. He proved a stickler for routine – one day a week was spent on manufacturing, whilst the rest was taken up selling his wares and keeping the books.

Thomas Beecham

In 1858 he moved to St Helens and rented a cottage in Milk Street. He now turned exclusively to the manufacturing and sale of pills.

His eldest son Joseph expanded the business, particularly by the use of advertising. In 1887, Thomas introduced the *Beecham's Music Portfolio* which was published for the next fifteen years. The advertisement 'Worth a Guinea a Box' appeared on the front, with the rest of the portfolio consisting of popular songs for family entertainment around the piano. It was a practical form of advertising which brought it into many homes; by 1902, 7,000,000 books had been sold.

Between 1865 and 1874 the order books show that sales went up from £2,500 to £16,338. By this time the pills could be purchased in every druggists in the country. Most of the money was ploughed back into the business, the rest going into his home, his art and the love of music. Eventually the retail side of the business was given up in favour of manufacturing. At this stage they sold approximately 1,000,000 pills a day, or 50 tons a year.

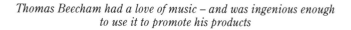

Thomas Beecham had a love of music – and was ingenious enough to use it to promote his products

Joseph Beecham was a true philanthropist, and he got good work from his staff by treating them hard but fairly.

In 1885 a new factory was built in St Helens – the clock tower standing 150 feet high was to become a famous landmark. Joseph sat on the electricity committee and the new factory was the first in the area to have electricity! Free cocoa and tea were provided; a billiards room, reading room and recreational ground were near at hand. In 1890 Joseph shortened the working day from 12 hours to 8 hours with 7 hours on Saturday.

Thomas Beecham died in 1907, the business being taken over by Joseph, but he died in 1916. The first public company was formed in 1924 , and at that time the business consisted of the main factory in St Helens with other factories in the USA, Canada and Australia. Up to this date the business consisted almost entirely of the sale of Beechams Pills. In October 1926, Beechams Powders were introduced.

In 1928 the company acquired a major holding in the Veno Drug Company, which had been founded in Manchester by the late Sir William Veno. In 1934 they acquired Phyllosan, and Phosferine was transferred to them in 1946. Setlers were introduced in 1957 and Cephos was acquired in 1959. The company is now part of SmithKline Beecham.

Beechams Pills were still 'Worth a Guinea a Box' in 1950

Bird's

TRADE MARK

In 1837, twenty-four year old Alfred Bird hung out a sign on a small shop in Bull Street, Birmingham: 'Alfred Bird F.C.S., Experimental Chemist'. It must have been doubly satisfying for him, firstly because it was his own business and secondly because he was doing something he genuinely enjoyed – experimental chemistry.

Colourful packs marketed in the Victorian period

Alfred had recently married Elizabeth, but unfortunately his new wife suffered digestive troubles. She was unable to tolerate eggs, or yeast-based products, including bread. It is thought she particularly liked custard (which even today is usually defined in dictionaries as 'a mixture of eggs and milk baked or served liquid'). It was Elizabeth's dyspepsia which directly stimulated Alfred into creating a number of what have since come to be known as convenience foods.

In 1843 he perfected a yeast substitute which he called Bird's Fermenting Powder, later known as baking powder. This was in no sense second-best; indeed tests soon showed that it produced superior bread, cakes and buns, ones of a much lighter texture than by the traditional use of live yeast.

But it was in his efforts to provide an eggless custard for his wife that Alfred Bird succeeded in developing a product which was to become almost synonymous with his company's name, and to be the foundation for a future major business. The new invention was based on cornflour and in many ways performed better than its natural counterpart. It had the advantage of being nutritious, palatable and inexpensive. It was simple to make and there was no danger of the custard turning into scrambled eggs in the saucepan!

After being introduced to a few of Alfred's immediate circle of customers, demand for his 'eggless custard' increased so rapidly that he had trouble keeping up with it.

Demand for the baking powder was slow by comparison, so Alfred Bird did

Alfred Bird had premises in Worcester Street, Birmingham, between 1847 and 1887

what many other manufacturers were to do in the future when a product did not move fast enough – he advertised. To make sure that people always had his advertisement in front of them, he extolled the virtues of his baking powder on calendars and then gave them away free. This is thought to be the first use of free calendars as advertising.

Later, he had the opportunity to prove that his baking powder could be used to supply the British troops with fresh bread instead of hard-tack biscuits. The head of the War Department, the Duke of Newcastle, agreed to sample bread made using only the new raising agent, baking powder. One of the loaves, stamped with the Birmingham Corporation seal, was sent to the duke who, after tasting it, proclaimed it 'sweet and good'. In due course Alfred Bird received an order for the supply of baking powder to H M Forces.

Alfred's eldest son, also Alfred, brought a new driving force to the little business. In those days most businesses had mottoes hung on the walls of the factory, exhorting workers to greater efforts. In their shop, by now in Worcester Street, the motto said simply:

'Early to Bed   Early to Rise
Stick to your Work   And Advertise'

The first pictorial advertisements began to appear in the 1880s. An early Birds advertisement was 'When the pie was opened the birds began to sing the praises of Bird's Custard'.

In 1868, Alfred Bird presented his son, Alfred Jnr, with a penny-farthing. It had wooden-spoke wheels and solid tyres and was one of many innova-tions he tried out. He was one of the first to use Charles Dunlop's new pneumatic tyres, and the record time for the

journey by tricycle from Lands End to John O'Groats is still in the name of Alfred Bird Jnr.

In the early 1870s, young Alfred devised and launched Bird's Blancmange Powder. When the product was launched there were no fewer than fourteen flavours. In 1895 came Bird's Jelly Crystals, the forerunner of the now well-known table jellies.

He offered his employees wages and conditions of service better than they could get anywhere else in Birming-ham, but in return he expected total dedication to his own inflexible standards of perfection.

Ah...cherries!
Big, luscious, ripe-and-ready-to-eat...

Ask your mother about Bird's! For as long as she can remember... and far, far longer... the name Bird's has stood for fine quality, utterly dependable and oh! such delicious foods.

with **BIRD'S CUSTARD**

...they're delicious!

Already the firm had registered its first trademark, 'The Ship on the World', believed to be one of the first to be registered under the new Trade Marks Act. In 1900 a new company, Alfred Bird and Sons Limited, was formed. The celebrated 'three birds' trademark was born in 1929.

In 1944 an approach was received from the General Foods Corporation of America, inviting Bird's to co-operate in the production in Britain of their food products, Grape Nuts and Maxwell House Ground Coffee. In 1947, Birds became part of the General Foods group.

During the years 1912–1915, an American fur trapper and biologist went out into the wilds of Labrador. Whilst on these expeditions he noticed that frozen fish and caribou meat tasted as good as fresh food, even after being frozen for many months. That man was Clarence Birdseye. His scientific training told him that slow freezing of fish or meat produced large ice crystals, which when thawed produced a very soggy material.

He gradually realised that in fact the speed of freezing was the all-important factor. In the sub-zero temperatures of Labrador, items left exposed to the elements almost immediately froze solid. He realised that during the quick-freezing process, many small ice crystals are formed, rather than a few larger ones in slower processes. The smaller crystals did not adversely affect the food in any way; the larger ones did.

In his laboratory at home he tried for eight years to recreate the effects of nature. It was not until the early 1920s that he came forward with a system of quick-freezing which was satisfactory and could be applied in a commercial world.

Clarence Birdseye, the father of the modern frozen food industry

In 1924, at Gloucester in Massachusetts, he started his company, the General Seafoods Corporation. Progress was very slow, so he sold the company and the rights of the system of quickfreezing to Postum Co, which later became the General Foods Corporation. Sales of frozen foods were slow to take off, but today the frozen food market is an enormous one, with Birds Eye in the United Kingdom (now under Unilever ownership) being the largest such company in the world. In 1981, Birds Eye and Wall's Ice Cream merged. The resultant company, known as Birds Eye Wall's, employs more than 5,000 people.

Today there is no dipping food into icy pools – it is now a very technologically based industry which produces a wide range of foods to consistently high standards.

Birds Eye food was 'The modern way to shop and cook' in 1959

Birdseye frozen peas from just after the Second World War – and more recently

In downtown Grand Rapids, Michigan, USA, Melville R Bissell and his wife Anna ran a crockery shop. The china was packed in sawdust and straw.

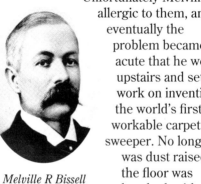

Melville R Bissell

Unfortunately Melville was allergic to them, and eventually the problem became so acute that he went upstairs and set to work on inventing the world's first workable carpet sweeper. No longer was dust raised as the floor was brushed; with Bissell's invention the dust and dirt was carried into the sweeper and retained there until its tray needed emptying. It was not so very different from the conventional sweepers of today, even incorporating a knob to

An early Bissell Sweeper – the Boudoir

adjust the brushes to meet the needs of the various depths of carpet pile. In September 1876, Melville obtained his patent and the Bissell Carpet Sweeper Company was born.

Everyone wanted one of these new sweepers, including Queen Victoria! It was to be another thirty years before the vacuum cleaner was invented.

The company continued to only make sweepers until the 1950s, when Melville's grandson introduced the first carpet shampoo machine, another bestseller right from the start. Today the company makes 500 different products in seven nations of the world.

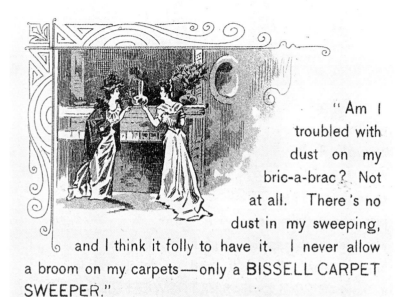

" Am I troubled with dust on my bric-a-brac? Not at all. There's no dust in my sweeping, and I think it folly to have it. I never allow a broom on my carpets—only a BISSELL CARPET SWEEPER."

" And you say that your bright carpets are due to your carpet sweeper? I'll have one to-morrow. I know that one sweeping with the old corn broom wears mine more than the cost of a BISSELL CARPET SWEEPER."

Bovril

Trademark Reg'd

The origins of Bovril drink can be traced back to 1871 when a Scot, John Lawson Johnston, started producing tinned beef in Canada to stock up French fortifications after the Franco-Prussian War. This enabled him to develop the blending of meat extract with caramel, salt and spices, something he had been experimenting with in a much smaller way. This product, a spread for putting on bread or mixing with water to make a hot drink, became known as 'Johnston's Fluid Beef' and later as 'Bo Vril'.

In 1884 after his Canadian factory had been destroyed by fire, Lawson Johnston returned to London and set up a factory at 10 Trinity Square. He started a vigorous and successful marketing campaign – even selling the product in public houses!

Above   *John Lawson Johnston developed and sold a 'fluid extract of beef'*

Left   *A 1909 testimonial from Antarctic explorer Sir Ernest Shackleton*

The first record of sales of Bovril drink in Britain was in 1886, with free tastings at the Colonial and Continental Exhibition in South Kensington.

The name originates from *bo* (latin for ox) and *vril* from Vrilya, the name given to 'life force' in Bulwer Lytton's long-forgotten novel *The Coming Race*. The founder of the company said that the name for Bovril drink came to him 'over a cigar'.

'**BOVRIL**' is a registered trademark of CPC International Inc

Shackleton says :

" *The question of the concentrated beef supply is most important— it must be Bovril.*"

Shackleton knows.   He is taking no risks.   He chooses Bovril because the food he takes must yield every ounce of nourishment to his men.

Follow Shackleton.   Into a single bottle of Bovril is packed the nourishment value of many pounds of beef, and over and above this, Bovril has the peculiar power of making other foods yield up much more of their nourishment to the body.

Now that times are difficult you can be sure of being nourished if you take Bovril.

It – <u>must</u> – be BOVRIL

Of all Stores, etc. at 1-oz. 25 c.;   2-oz. 40 c.;   4-oz. 70 c.;   8-oz. $1.30;   16-oz. $2.25.
Bovril Cordial, large, $1 25;   5-oz. 40 c.   16-oz. Johnston's Fluid Beef (Vimbos), $1.20.

S.H.B.

*A favourite old poster,
which first appeared in 1915 and was
revived in the early twenties*

*William Britain founded
'the world's biggest private army'*

William Britain was a Birmingham man who moved to London around the middle of the last century. He was a brilliant toy maker and produced walking bears, Chinese coolies drawing rickshaws, men on penny-farthing bicycles and Scotsmen who drank a glass of liquor with the aid of a clockwork fly-wheel momentum which was coin-operated or worked by hand. He also made a toy steam-roller which worked by the principle on which all the modern friction, or 'push along' toys, are based.

Unfortunately these toys were expensive and appealed only to a small market. William wanted to enlarge his scope and looked at the situation in Germany, where solid lead soldiers were produced in large numbers and sold all over the world. They were

heavy and also expensive. William invented a new method of hollow casting models, which were lighter, cheaper and, due to his attention to detail, more like the real thing.

In 1893 he made a model of a Life Guard, not much more than two inches high, and it was probably this, more than anything else, which led to what has been called 'the world's biggest private army'. Today the early models – originally sold at a halfpenny for foot soldiers and a penny or twopence for horse soldiers – are cherished collectors' pieces.

The creator of the army lived in a Victorian house in Lambeth Road, Hornsey in north London. His sons and daughters worked with him, the

sons doing the meticulous research which goes into the preparation of each model, the daughters painting them. The house was later converted into a factory and soon 200,000 soldiers were 'marching' out each week.

Today plastic has taken the place of metal, but still the soldier is produced to the standard 1/32nd scale. The colouring on such tiny models is essentially hand work, mainly done by outworkers, military band instruments being either gold or silver plated.

Today these tiny model figures are exported to 52 countries worldwide from the new factory in Walthamstow, London.

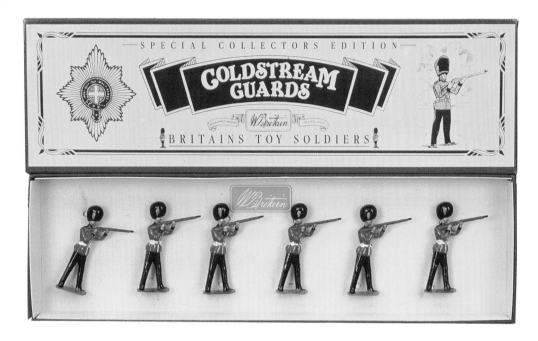

Brooke Bond

Arthur Brooke . . . but no Mr Bond

Arthur Brooke was born in 1845, son of a wholesale tea merchant, above the shop in George Street, Ashton-under-Lyne, Lancashire. At the age of nineteen years he was taken on at the Liverpool branch of a wholesale tea company. As a result of hard work he was transferred to the company's head office in London. However, he heard that his father was spoiling the company and so he returned home and joined his father in the business. He threw all his energies into the work and opened up new branches all over Lancashire. Soon he had saved over £400 from his share of the profits and he decided to set up his own company.

He opened a shop at 29 Market Street in Manchester, because it was opposite the Royal Exchange and in a street that was always busy with housewives. In 1869 he opened the doors and put over the shop the name 'Brooke, Bond and Company'. There was no Mr Bond; the name 'seemed to him to sound well'. He was twenty-four years old; this was the foundation of his business, selling tea, coffee and sugar for cash only over the counter. He developed premium blends of tea, selecting exact proportions from the best of several teas. His teas were always reliable, always packed so as to give full weight. He was a vigorous salesman – his teas were 'Deliciously Rich', 'Ripe, Juicy, Fragrant', and 'the Creme de la Creme'.

Arthur Brooke prospered and he opened further shops in Liverpool, Leeds and Bradford. In 1872 he moved to London where he took over a warehouse. Unfortunately a trade depression hit Britain in the late

Always <u>refreshes</u>, always <u>revives</u>– your cup of P.G. Tips

CHANGE TO BROOKE BOND P.G. TIPS—*the tea you can really taste*

PG Tips in the early 1960s

1870s, particularly the industrial north. It was typical of Arthur Brooke that his first action was to reduce his own standard of living, selling his house and giving up his carriage and horses.

Another retail grocer asked whether he might buy Brooke Bond's blended tea in bulk at wholesale prices. Arthur Brooke realised more grocers might also be interested and so he advertised

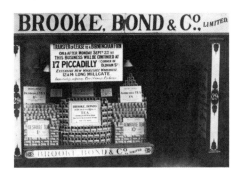

The shop at 29 Market Street, Manchester, where Brooke Bond began. The shop stayed with the company for twenty-eight years

wholesale supplies of blended tea – cash with order. The orders came flooding in and once again the firm began to prosper. In 1892 the firm became 'Brooke Bond and Company Limited'. The business had become primarily wholesale, built on three basic factors: intelligent buying of tea, sensible blending to satisfy the market and clever advertising to attract custom.

From his first visit to America, Arthur Brooke was an enthusiast for novelty and for modern methods of salesmanship. On the side of corner shops in the North of England, they fixed tin advertising plates.

In the 1930s the Co-operative Wholesale Society – the Co-op – was the giant of the tea trade in Britain, and during the days of the depression, low wages and the dole, the 'divi' (dividend) was very welcome.

The manager of Brooke Bond's Manchester shop said, 'If only we could offer a dividend'. They set to work, producing a good economical blend, planning the packaging, promotion, and drawing up a 'dividend card' consisting of 60 squares. The production of a label incorporating a perforated, detachable, gummed stamp was not easy, but it was achieved. Customers would save their stamps, each valued at 1d, and hand in their completed cards to the grocer to be given 5s. The stamp on each packet bore a drawing of a beehive, the symbol of thrift. 'Dividend' tea was launched in November 1935, and was soon a bestseller.

Tea was also sometimes sold on its medicinal qualities – it was said to be an aid to digestion – but legal objections were made to the use of the word 'digestive' in association with tea. Brooke Bond invented the name Pre-Gest-Te, bulk packets of it bearing the letters 'PG', the tea becoming known to the trade as 'PG Tips', eventually being adopted as its brand name.

In 1954, picture cards were inserted in the packets of tea. By 1968 the annual distribution of these cards had exceeded 720 million. The company's advertising agents suggested that chimpanzees, associated with tea over many years through the 'chimps' tea party at London Zoo, might be used to make an amusing and unusual television commercial. The first of these appeared at Christmas 1956. Soon the Brooke Bond chimpanzees were in demand for public appearances and drew large crowds wherever they appeared.

In the 1960s the company entered the tea-bag market, and when vending machines came into greater use in factories and offices the company started to provide a comprehensive service.

Brooke Bond's tea factory at Aldgate, London, earlier this century

As a result of its merger with Liebig in 1968, Brooke Bond became joint owners of cattle ranches in Argentina, Paraguay and Rhodesia. The company is now known as Brooke Bond Oxo.

Cadbury

In 1824 a young Quaker, John Cadbury, opened a shop at 93 Bull Street, Birmingham, chiefly for the sale of tea and coffee. The family's connection with the Society of Friends had begun in the earliest days of the Quaker movement.

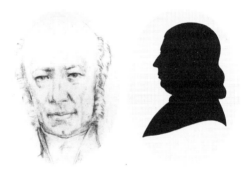

John Cadbury (left) *and Joseph Fry*

Medical literature of the eighteenth century recommended chocolate for its beneficial qualities. Manufacturers quickly realised that this supposed therapeutic potion could be made into a particularly pleasant and palatable drink. The cocoa beans were roasted over an open charcoal fire, winnowed by hand, ground and crushed on a heated slab. The ground mass was then mixed with flavourings and sugar in copper or tin pans, and the final tablets were shaped by hand and cooled on tins before final packaging. At that time, eating chocolate was virtually unknown and production consisted of making tablets of chocolate, which the consumer placed at the bottom of a chocolate cup and added water or milk.

In John Cadbury's early days the sale of cocoa and chocolate was merely a sideline. He roasted his own cocoa beans and ground them by hand with a pestle and mortar. He was an energetic man with an eye for business and display; he had a Chinese figurine in native costume serving at his tea counter, and in his shop there was always something to attract and hold the attention of customers.

On a domestic scale he mastered the essentials of cocoa and chocolate making which he and his successors were to develop and perfect. If sugar was included, the product was labelled 'chocolate'; if not, it was 'cocoa'.

His trading in drinking chocolates and cocoas was so successful that in 1831 he rented a small factory in Crooked Lane, near to his shop. Here he developed the manufacturing side of his business. He devoted himself firstly to his shop, then his factory, but he was also a pioneer in smoke abatement as well as being active in religious and philanthropic work.

The nearest approach to the highly refined cocoa powder of today was the so-called 'Soluble Cocoa' (it did not really dissolve, but remained in a fine suspension in the liquid); almost all the products which he made were for drinking. By 1842 he was selling 16 different sorts of chocolate and 11 cocoas; chocolate for eating was still a novelty. The retail business was given up in 1849 in order to concentrate on manufacturing. In 1853 they received the royal warrant and have held such warrants ever since.

When the business passed into the hands of John's sons, Richard and George, in 1861, they set about reorganising it and lifting it out of a period of decline. In 1866 they started making pure cocoa known as Cadbury's 'Cocoa Essence', being

The Bournville factory in 1879

advertised as 'Absolutely Pure – Therefore Best'. At first it was a hard struggle to establish the new line, opponents contending that it had lost its nourishing qualities.

By the late 1870s the partners were looking for new premises and decided

FRY'S MILK CHOCOLATE

DESPERATION. PACIFICATION. EXPECTATION. ACCLAMATION. REALIZATION. "IT'S FRY'S"

J.S. FRY & SONS LTD BRISTOL & LONDON.

The classic 'Five Boys' advert

to move into the country. The Bournbrook Estate came on the market in 1878. It was four miles south-west of Birmingham, near to a railway and canal, and between two main roads; it also had a good water supply. The brothers bought 14½ acres of the estate. Originally it had been intended to call the factory the Bournbrook Works. Early on, however, the name was changed to Bournville – a prejudice in favour of French chocolate. At the time, French confectionery was highly prized, so *ville* (French for town) was added to Bourne, and became anglicised as Bournville. The new factory was taken over in 1879, but since then the floor space has been increased 40 or 50 fold and the original site has been extended to 47 acres. Further neighbouring land has

been converted into works recreation grounds, much of which has subsequently been built on. George Cadbury built houses near the works for key workers, and in 1893 he bought a further 120 acres of land near the works on which he built in harmony with the infant Garden City movement. In 1900 he handed over his land and houses to the Bournville Village Trust, with the proviso that the revenue from the property was to be devoted to the extension of the estate and the promotion of housing reform.

Cadbury Brothers made their first milk chocolate in 1897. The early Bournville product was similar to the dark variety then being imported from

Switzerland. Experiments went on at Bournville, and as a result a 'light' chocolate, containing more milk, was introduced in 1905. This chocolate, made with fresh full cream milk, was named Cadbury's Dairy Milk. Its sales increased rapidly, breaking the Swiss monopoly of the milk chocolate market, to become the best selling moulded chocolate bar in the UK.

Bournville Cocoa, with its distinctive 'chocolaty' flavour, was introduced in 1908.

Plain Tray was introduced in 1914, and the milk chocolate version, in its distinctive purple box with gold script, appeared a year later.

Workers were always thought of as part of the family, and in 1918, democratically elected works councils were set up, one for men and another for women employees. These councils were concerned with working conditions, training and the social life of the employees, and continued for over half a century.

In 1919, Cadbury Brothers merged with J S Fry & Sons of Bristol. The history of Fry extends through ten reigns, from George II to Elizabeth II. Walter Churchman, who had premises in Bristol in 1728, invented a water engine which he used to make chocolate. In 1731 he was granted a letters patent for:

'The sole use of an engine by him invented for the expeditious, fine and clean making of chocolate to greater perfection than by any other method in use, the patentee purposes to sell his chocolate at common prices.'

When Walter Churchman's son died in 1761, Joseph Fry took this opportunity to expand his trade and purchased the patent. Joseph, a Quaker, was born in 1728 and settled in Bristol when he was about twenty years old. In the autumn of 1756 he announced in the local press:

'The best sorts of chocolate made and sold wholesale and retail by Joseph Fry, Apothecary, in Small Street, Bristol.'

This advertisement is one of the earliest associations of the name Fry with chocolate.

In 1822, Joseph's three grandsons, Joseph, Francis and Richard, constituted the firm of 'J. S. Fry & Sons', the name it has borne ever since. Between 1860 and 1907, Fry opened seven more factories in Bristol. No doubt the increased demand was at least partly due to the introduction of the now famous chocolate cream bar in 1866, and the first true milk chocolate, which was commercially developed in 1902. Fry became a registered private company in 1896, having

Cadbury's Cocoa Essence, 'Absolutely pure – therefore best'

seven directors, all members of the Fry family, and 4,500 employees.

Turkish Delight was introduced in 1914, Crunchie in 1929, and up to 1938 no less than 189 new lines were introduced.

In 1921, the entire Fry business was transferred from Bristol to a new site, now known as Somerdale, at Keynsham midway between Bristol and Bath. The name Somerdale was chosen as a result of a national competition in 1923, and the site there extends over many acres of countryside.

The merger of Cadbury in 1969 with Schweppes and subsequent developments have led to Cadbury Schweppes taking the lead in both the confectionery and soft drinks markets in the UK. Cadbury Schweppes now manufactures products in 60 countries and trades in over 120 worldwide.

Clarks

Joseph Clark was a yeoman farmer and a pillar of the Street (a village in Somerset) Quaker meeting. In 1821 his son, Cyrus, joined a Quaker neighbour, Arthur Clothier, in the business of tanning, fell-mongering and wool stapling. At the same time, Cyrus began tanning sheep-skins with the wool on for making sheepskin rugs. In 1825 the partnership split up, Cyrus taking over the fell-mongering, wool-stapling and rug business. The firm of Clarks had begun.

After three years, when James Clark was seventeen years old, the business looked promising enough for him also

Cyrus and James Clark, founders of the firm

to have a place in it, and he was apprenticed on characteristically strict terms. He paid £80 for the privilege, received no wages, and undertook to avoid both marriage and games of

chance for five years! In return he lived with his brother's family for free. He took home skins that were unfit for rugs because of the shortness of their wool and cut them into pieces for cottagers to make up as slippers.

In an astonishingly short time, with the addition of lambswool socks, boots and welted shoes, comparative profits from footwear rose above those from the business's original activities. Already, in 1833, shoes and socks accounted for about a third of total sales, and James, being now free from his apprenticeship, was accepted into partnership by Cyrus.

Cyrus and James travelled all over the country to sell their product. Ireland was an important area, taking nearly a third of their footwear as early as 1836. Exports, to as far away as Australia, were mainly in the hands of agents in London. All shoes were stamped with the individual maker's number, to make possible a scrupulous system of checking. In 1842, 12,000 pairs of all kinds of footwear were produced.

From 1925

Although a factory was built in 1829, most work continued to be done at home. Sometimes whole families worked together to make enough for a week's necessities. Wives learned to rock their babies' cradles with their feet while they stitched uppers. With his pincers, knife, hammer, awls, tacks and rivets of brass or wood, the man of the house made the complete shoes. In winter they worked round the light of one central candle; more light would have wasted money!

It suited the Clarks that their employees should be industrious and sober – the best way of ensuring this was for the Clarks themselves to be industrious and sober. James Clark believed he was 'the first to sign any Temperance Pledge anywhere south of Bristol'.

Clarks bought three treadle sewing machines in 1856 for closing uppers. Two years later they imported machines for cutting soles. By 1880 the only process not to have been mechanised was the lasting. However, ready-made shoes had come into their own. In 1883 the Hygienic range was launched, which gave consideration to foot-shape and development and has hardly been surpassed even today. In the 1880s, branding became essential to cope with competition. By now Clarks had 620 styles, mainly women's and children's.

In the 1930s, competitors moved into the retail trade by buying up shops, but Clarks did not want to alienate independent shops and resisted following their competitors. However,

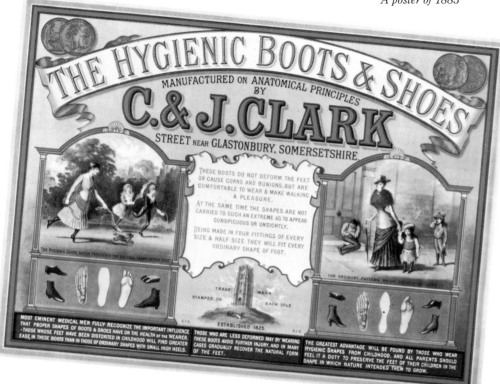

'Lady's bar shoe, beaded glacé kid', from their 1895 catalogue

in 1937 they bought up part of the Abbot chain; they did not put up their own name but the name of Peter Lord. Why Peter Lord? Clarks wanted a name for the new company – a name that was easy to remember, one that would strike the eye, one that had a pleasing balance. The surname 'Lord' served as a good foundation, and 'Peter' harmonised happily with it – and so 'Peter Lord' was duly christened.

During the Second World War, production of children's sandals was stepped up as they were ideal for the thousands of evacuees to rural settings. Torpedo parts were also made in the factory, to help the war effort.

To cope with the demand after the war, factories were founded outside Street for the first time, the first one, St Johns of Bridgewater, producing sandals in 1945. Other factories soon followed. New technology, such as the CEMA process which directly vulcanised rubber onto the leather upper, revolutionised the industry.

Clarks has expanded overseas, and there are sales to countries around the world.

Coca-Cola

Coca-Cola all began, according to legend, in modest surroundings in Atlanta, Georgia, USA, where in 1886 a pharmacist, Dr John S Pemberton, first produced a syrup in a three-legged pot in his back yard. The new product was placed on sale for five cents a glass as a soda fountain drink on the 8th May 1886. The first sales were at Jacob's Pharmacy in the heart of downtown Atlanta.

Dr John S Pemberton first produced Coca-Cola in a three-legged pot in his back yard

The first advert proclaimed that Coca-Cola was 'delicious and refreshing'. It was Dr Pemberton's partner, Frank Robinson, who suggested the name and wrote 'Coca-Cola' in flowing script.

For the next eight months only 13 drinks per day were sold, not a very auspicious beginning for a product whose sales now average more than 600 million drinks a day! Dr Pemberton did not realise the importance of the beverage he had created. In need of funds because of ill-health, he gave two Atlanta friends a two-thirds interest for $1,220, including the sole right to manufacture the syrup. Four months before Dr Pemberton died in 1888, he and his son accepted $500 for all remaining rights to the product from Asa G Candler, who had come to Atlanta fifteen years earlier with $1.75 in his pocket. Later he started to buy up other rights and eventually gained complete control.

The trademark 'Coca-Cola' was registered in the United States in 1893. Candler, a firm believer in advertising, gave away thousands of complimentary coupons for a free glass of Coca-Cola. He also carried out a large promotional programme, giving away souvenir fans, calendars, clocks, urns and countless novelties.

Joseph A Biedenharn was so impressed by the growing demand for Coca-Cola at his soda fountain in Vicksburg, Mississippi that he installed bottling machinery in the rear of the store and began to take bottles of Coca-Cola around to plantations and lumber camps up and down the river. He was the first man to put Coca-Cola in bottles using syrup shipped from Atlanta. Thirty years later there were a thousand bottling plants in the USA.

A 1910 advert

It was in the first year of the twentieth century that Coca-Cola was first served in London. Howard Candler, son of the company's founder, took a jug of syrup on a holiday trip and an order for five gallons of the syrup was sent back to the USA.

The first sales were at Jacob's Pharmacy, Atlanta, in May 1886

Imitation has always been a problem, and one way of preventing this was the introduction of a distinctive bottle. Its unique shape was granted a registration as a trademark by the US Patent Office in 1960.

Company president Robert Winship Woodruff had the vision of Coca-Cola becoming an international drink, and in 1926 he formed a foreign sales department. He also developed the six bottle carton in the early 1920s, an innovation at the time. Packaging of Coca-Cola in cans began in 1955.

When the Apollo astronauts returned from their moonflight they were greeted by a Times Square sign flashing: 'Welcome back to Earth, Home of Coca-Cola'.

'COCA-COLA' and 'COKE' are registered trademarks which identify the same product of The Coca-Cola Company

Colman's *of Norwich*

Jeremiah Colman had been flour milling on the outskirts of Mousehold Heath near Norwich. In 1814 he leased a mill about four miles south of Norwich at Stoke Holy Cross, on the River Tas. An earlier owner had used it for paper making as well as the milling of flour, but his successor had started to make mustard. Jeremiah Colman had to choose between paper making, or flour and mustard milling. He chose mustard and flour.

The Colman family were well known in the area, having been involved in agriculture for many years. However, Jeremiah had no family of his own, but he adopted his brother's eldest child, James. James was later joined in the business by two other brothers, Jeremiah and Edward.

Twenty years after starting his business, James was still mixing and sifting the mustard flours obtained from the crushed seed, sometimes needing the help of his wife and daughter. They also ground wheat and in 1830 started to manufacture starch from the wheat.

Even in those early days the firm's social concerns was very much to the front – Mrs Jeremiah Colman ran a clothing club, adding a bonus to the sums which members paid in. At Christmas a dinner was held in the granary.

In 1854 the first mill rose on the Carrow site on the south side of Norwich near the junction of the rivers Yare and Wensum. The first mill was the Mustard Mill, but flour and starch mills also appeared along the river-bank. In the centre of these factory buildings was the counting house, where the administrative staff were located.

The famous Colman bull's head dates back to 1855, and the Colmans signature appearing on mustard labels was written by Edward Colman, one of the three nephews of the founder, Jeremiah.

Once again their social welfare came to the forefront. In 1857 they established a new school for the children of the Carrow employees; parents paid a fee of 1d a week for the first child and 1/2d for others of their family, the money actually going towards the cost of prizes – the firm paid all the costs. In 1868, Mrs Colman started a meals service for the workers who could not go home for their midday meals; for 4d they had hot meat, vegetable stew and a pint of coffee. A dispensary with a nurse was added in 1864. Shortly afterwards the women also gained a trained nurse, the first record of an industrial nurse in this country.

Jeremiah Colman

During all this development at Carrow, Jeremiah James Colman, the son of James, had been very much in charge of the company. He was a very dominating character, not only in the company but also in the city, becoming its mayor in 1868 and a Member of Parliament in 1871.

The Colman bull's head trade mark was registered in 1855, originally for a 'Starch for Laundry and Manufacturing Purposes'

JEREMIAH JAMES COLMAN, JEREMIAH COLMAN, and FREDERICK EDWARD COLMAN, trading under the style of J. and J. COLMAN, Cannon Street, London, and Norwich ; Mustard, Starch, Corn Flour, and Blue Manufacturers.

| 4 | Starch for Laundry and Manufacturing Purposes. | 90 | 3rd Jan. 1876. | Seven years before 3rd Jan. 1876. |

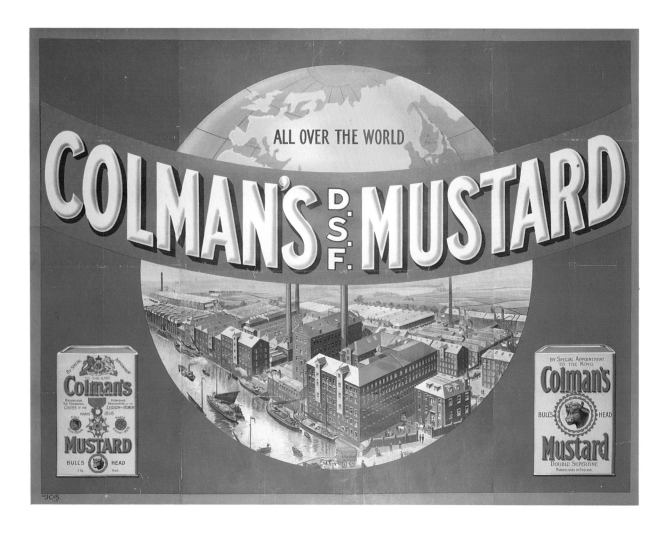

In 1896 the partnership became a limited company, Jeremiah James Colman becoming the first chairman.

On the death of J J Colman, Frederick Edward held the chairmanship, but with his early death it was taken up by yet another Jeremiah, J J Colman's son, and he held the position for forty-two years.

In 1903, Colmans took over Keen Robinson for their mustard and spice trade, but in so doing found that they had become one of the most important manufacturers of baby food in the country. Even today Robinsons is well known for its baby food and soft drinks.

In 1936, Robinson's Lemon Barley Water was introduced, to be followed by other fruit flavours. In 1938, J & J Colman became part of a greater organisation, Reckitt & Colman.

Colmans advertising is a story in itself, and includes not just packaging but also mustard pots, mirrors, tins, booklets and wallcharts. Indeed a visit to the Mustard Shop in Bridewell Alley, Norwich, is a tourist's must.

DAMART

In the French town of Roubaix in the 1950s, three brothers, members of the Despature family, had a weaving business manufacturing fine woollen cloths. At about that time they were experimenting with a new man-made chlorofibre which possessed remarkable insulation and water repellent properties. In common with other synthetic fibres it also generated tribo-electricity, a form of static electricity generated when fibres rub together

Below *Catalogues through the years*
Right *Thermal underwear being worn (underneath!) on the British Transglobe Expedition 1979–81*

during wear – this is said, by some people, to have therapeutic value in the treatment of rheumatism, arthritis and muscular complaints.

The brothers' genius lay in recognising its application in the knitting of fabrics superbly suited to underwear. After rigorous testing and development, 'Thermolactyl' was created.

Legend has it that the brothers met at a cafe opposite Rue Dammartine to discuss their breakthrough – hence the name Damart.

Today this unique fibre is imported into Britain under licence, as indeed also happens in many countries around the globe, where it is knitted into the wide range of garments. Its versatility has increased as it has been found to mix well with other fibres like silk to produce luxury and warmth in

the same garment, used in a range of ladies underwear and nightwear.

Whilst Damart's garments are ideal for our winter conditions, this does not really put the garments to the test! Damart's garments have been successfully used on Everest, including being used in the highest overnight bivouac in mountaineering history; and at the Arctic and Antarctic.

And the 'flash' in the company logo – it symbolises the tribo-electricity!

In 1965 Damart came to Bingley, on the banks of the River Aire in West Yorkshire, and it is from there that the famous Thermolactyl underwear, and other garments, have gone to many parts of the world.

JOHN DICKINSON

John Dickinson was born in 1782, the eldest son of Captain Thomas Dickinson RN. When John was nearly fifteen years old he was apprenticed to Thomas Harrison, stationer of London, for seven years. He started his own business in 1801, and by 1806 he was supplying the East India Company with paper on a considerable scale.

So far John had traded as a middle-man, selling paper made by others.

One of the first Dickinson adverts, from June 1890

The art of paper-making had changed little since the first English mill had been set up in 1490 – it still consisted of the essential processes of reducing rags to fibre by boiling, bleaching the resultant pulp, then depositing it on wire cloth while suspended in water. As early as 1797, Nicholas Louis Robert made a small model for the manufacture of paper on an endless web – he had invented the first practical paper machine.

John Dickinson embarked on making a rival machine. In 1809 he obtained a patent and in the same year he acquired Apsley Mill in Hemel Hempstead, a very old converted flour mill. Dickinson had very little capital of his own but took as a partner George Longman, a member of the famous publishing family. He was wealthier and older, so the firm traded as Longman and Dickinson. Ten years later they were supplying the King's Printers with paper for an edition of the Bible.

Home Park Mills was built in 1826 and around it were built cottages for the workpeople. Just as it was completed the East India Company gave him an order for 10,000 reams, a real piece of good fortune.

It was the age of the penny post, and Dickinson became interested in Rowland Hill's idea of stamped covers. Hill suggested that Dickinson might

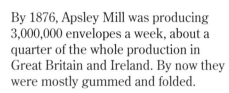

John Dickinson (c1860)

be given a government contract to supply them with paper for such covers. In August 1839 the Lords of the Treasury issued a proclamation asking for ideas as to how 'the stamp may best be brought into use'. John Dickinson spent three months improving his threaded paper. William Mulready recommended an envelope, to be sold flat and ungummed, with an elaborate engraved design to prevent forgery. Dickinson secured a grant for Post Office covers, and the first proofs were submitted to the queen on the 3rd April 1840.

By 1876, Apsley Mill was producing 3,000,000 envelopes a week, about a quarter of the whole production in Great Britain and Ireland. By now they were mostly gummed and folded.

Basildon Bond was introduced in 1911. It belonged to Millington & Sons, a company which later became part of the Dickinson Group. It was the first 'bond' notepaper, gaining its name from a meeting of directors at a house party near Basildon in Berkshire. Looking round the district, one of them spotted the name Basildon, and realised that it had just the right allit-erative quality needed when associ-ated with the nature of the paper. They decided there and then on the name. Basildon Bond very quickly became known as a quality writing paper.

In the early 1940s, Klaus Maertens and Herbert Funck met whilst students in Munich and a close friendship developed between them. Klaus became an orthopaedic surgeon, whilst Herbert gained his doctorate in engineering.

In 1945, Dr Maertens had an accident whilst skiing and damaged his foot. The injury caused him considerable pain, particularly when walking in conventional shoes. It was as a result of this discomfort, using the medical knowledge of Klaus and the technical experience of Herbert, that they developed an air-cushioned sole.

By 1947 the first shoes with air-cushioned soles were being produced. This was no modern factory product but rather one where they used redundant materials at the end of the war, and also used 'amateurs' to manufacture them. The materials were sponge rubber and Igelit, a material used to repair the bodies of early aircraft, which was 'welded' around the sponge rubber, thus producing a smooth sole. The 'amateurs' included an organ builder, a carpenter, a locksmith, a musician and a tailor. All the shoes were made without nails and were almost indestructable.

Work commenced in the German town of Seeshaupt near Munich. The shoes carried Dr Maertens' name, and were patented from the earliest days. News of this new product spread across the Continent and by the mid 1950s they were achieving a reasonable success, although modest by today's standards.

In the late 1950s the right to manufacture Dr Maertens was offered to all the

Dr Klaus Maertens (left) *and Herbert Funck*

large UK manufacturers, none of whom considered the process to be more than a gimmick.

However, one man did see the true potential; he was William Griggs. The company of R Griggs & Co Ltd had been founded in 1901 by William's father, Reginald, in Wollaston, a village in the shoe-making county of Northamptonshire. Bill secured the exclusive rights to manufacture in the United Kingdom for a trial year, at the end of which the relationship was confirmed for the future. The name was anglicised to Dr Martens, and an in-house brand name of 'AirWair' was created.

The first Dr Martens boot came off the UK production line in 1960, and by the end of the decade they had become something of a cult in Britain, being accepted as functional workwear and as a street fashion.

Today the sole is made of an oil-based PVC granular compound which is resistant to oil, fat, acid, petrol and alkali, moulded into a carefully developed slip-limiting pattern and attached to the upper with invisible Goodyear stitching.

These huge fibreglass boots (just over 4ft 6in tall) were specially made for Elton John to wear in the rock opera Tommy, *and are now owned by R Griggs & Co*

Lucian Ercolani came to England from Italy, where he was born, in 1888. His father was a picture frame maker, and when young Lucian should have been at school he was often seen cycling round London selling the frames.

Lucian Ercolani

But Lucian had patience mixed with enthusiasm, and was keen to gain the skills of the cabinet maker. At the age of fourteen he started going to night school to study art and cabinet making. In 1911 he took up an appointment at High Wycombe Technical School as a teacher of art, with particular reference to furniture design. Whilst he was teaching in the evenings, in the daytime he was working, gaining wider experience and money – money to start his own business.

In 1920 he bought a meadow, large enough to accommodate a factory. His first step was to sell the turf; then he designed his own building, without the help of an architect (his original sketch hangs in the company's board-room), and pegged out the site with his own hands.

Many people were sceptical of Mr Ercolani's project and called it 'Erkie's Folly'. He had no capital, but he found others to invest in his project. However, what he lacked in money he made up for in ideas, and he had the courage and initiative to put ideas into practice. He was determined to make furniture to the highest standards, linking craftsmanship with mechanisation.

After the Second World War the Ercol Company created a style which was unique, using methods of construction which would discourage others from copying them. In 1947 an amazed furniture world saw the first production-line Windsor chair – Ercol were now able to produce one of these quality chairs every twenty seconds, and the finished product was better than the hand-made one!

His design principle was to make the best of modern furniture, inspired by the best of the past. It also seemed desirable to use British materials, such as elm, beech and ash. With elm he had to eliminate the problems of distortion; this he did by stacking it in the open air for one to two years and then kiln drying it for 10–14 days.

To ensure those original standards are maintained, the company has its own craft school within the works. As a mark of those standards, the Worshipful Company of Furniture Makers has granted the company their guild mark for volume production, having been previously awarded only for single pieces. Today as an independent company it exports to Japan, Australia, America, Canada, and Europe.

The Windsor Chair advertised in 1953

The trade in bananas has its origins in the seventeenth century, with some small ships calling at either the Canary Islands or Madeira on their way back to Europe. By the 1870s a tiny business had grown up, but bananas were still an expensive luxury on the London market.

Edward Fyffe

The Fyffe family had been engaged in the tea business since the reign of James I, and Ebenezer Wathen Fyffe had taken control in 1849. Ebenezer's younger son, Edward Wathen Fyffe, married a Miss Brown in the early 1880s, and they had two daughters. These two confinements, so close together, left her in a very weak state and she was advised to convalesce in a warm climate. In accordance with this advice they spent most of 1887 in the Canary Islands and she made a full recovery. Edward saw the cheap and plentiful supply of bananas, and investigated the possibility of shipping the fruit to London. He decided to provide an import agency in London, thus putting the onus on the growers to provide saleable fruit. The first small consignment of about sixty bunches arrived at Fyffe's office in September 1888. It sold at Covent Garden at an excellent profit. Shipments became more regular, and the top-quality fruit was sold to high-class fruiterers in the city, with the over-ripe or inferior fruit going to barrow-boys.

By 1897 the venture had proved so successful that the growers' syndicate in the Canary Islands decided to buy out the agency. Edward Wathen Fyffe retired the same year at the age of forty-four and took no further part in the industry, although his name has remained synonymous with the banana in Britain. He died in 1935.

In 1901, Elders and Fyffes was formed, partly to cope with large consignments of bananas being imported from Jamaica. The journey from Jamaica was much longer than from the Canary Islands and arrangements had to be made for the fruit to be kept

Like this FYFFES but Blue

Look for this Blue Label when you buy bananas. It appears on every hand of Fyffes' bananas. The Blue Label protects you and guarantees that you really are getting

FYFFES BANANAS

fresh, cool-air systems being fitted to over a hundred ships. By 1912 they were responsible for the importation of 6 million of the 7 million bunches which came into Britain that year.

An early Fyffes window display

Thus, Fyffes became the first 'branded' fruit in the world.

In 1929, Fyffes introduced the famous blue label on their bunches of bananas. They also promoted their wares by many ingenious stunts and devices, using its slogan 'Bananas, The All-Food Fruit'. By this time, they were importing about 12 million stems a year, so the placing of the blue labels, each of which had to be individually wetted and put in position, was quite a major task.

Today, Fyffes is a multinational company, growing, shipping, ripening and distributing bananas to retailers in both the UK and Ireland. The business has grown beyond bananas, however, and distribution depots in both countries supply retailers with a whole range of quality fruits and vegetables.

STANLEY GIBBONS

Edward Stanley Gibbons was born in 1840 – an appropriate year for a boy destined for such a future, for it was the year the world's first postage stamp was produced in Britain. He was the youngest son of William Gibbons, a pharmaceutical chemist, who lived in Plymouth. Their home was above the shop.

Around 1854, when stamp collecting was just beginning, he had a little book containing about twenty stamps. At the age of fifteen years he left school and entered the local Naval Bank as a junior clerk. However, before he had hardly settled down in this job, his elder brother died and Edward had to take his place as an apprentice in pills and potions. It was at this time that his love for stamps developed.

In between prescriptions, he had ample opportunity to follow his interest. In 1856, his father, who recognised the potential of the stamp dealing, set aside a desk in the shop from which he could deal exclusively in stamps. He had an undeniable business acumen, and it was not long before the business had prospered to such an extent that a room above the shop was set aside for it. At first the business was called 'E S Gibbons', but this was soon changed to 'E Stanley Gibbons', and later still to 'Stanley, Gibbons and Company' – dignity and importance were conferred by the insertion of the comma!

Eventually the stamp business grew so much that its turnover exceeded that of the pharmacy, which passed to Stanley Gibbons on the death of his father. He sold the pharmacy and concentrated on stamp trading. It was shortly after this that fortune smiled generously on him. One morning in 1863, two sailors came into the shop with a kit bag full of Cape of Good Hope triangulars. The sailors had won the stamps in a raffle during shore leave in Cape Town and were pleased to accept a £5 note for the whole bagful. It is not difficult to imagine the excitement and pleasure this purchase gave Stanley Gibbons; he estimated the profit from this deal alone at £500.

He now began to import unused stamps from all over the world. His brother, Commander A F Gibbons RN, brought parcels of stamps back to Plymouth from his voyages. Another remarkable incident was when the postmaster of Albany in Western Australia forwarded

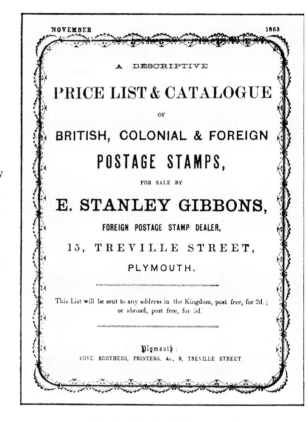

The first Stanley Gibbons catalogue (November 1865)

£20 worth of unused stamps, remarking that he had taken the liberty of sending 120 of the 2d printed in the colours of the 6d, for which he was obliged to charge 6d as he had been charged that by the authorities. These were the rare mauve 2d stamps of 1879, with colour error, now priced at over £5,000 each.

In 1865 the prototype of the famous catalogue was published in the form of a monthly price list. By 1870 the price

Stanley Gibbons at the time of his retirement in 1890

list was appearing as an embryo catalogue in book form, and at the same time he published his first stamp album.

In 1874 he took the biggest step of his career. He moved his business to London, confining himself almost

The modern range of Stanley Gibbons products

entirely to a correspondence business, sometimes handling 200–300 letters a day. He personally edited all the albums and catalogues, working entirely on his own.

In 1890 he retired, with a considerable fortune, his business being bought by Charles J Phillips, a part-time stamp dealer. Gibbons gave him the task of valuing the vast stock, and accepted

his offer of £25,000. Gibbons remained as chairman of the new limited company and Charles Phillips became managing director.

The new company expanded at an amazing rate, and on the 20th July 1890 a house magazine, thought to be the first ever published, was born. It was called the *Monthly Journal*, the forerunner to *Gibbons Stamp Monthly*.

In March 1891 they moved to half a shop at 435 Strand, but the firm once more outgrew its premises and a further shop, the world-famous 391 Strand, was leased. These premises were to become the philatelic centre of the entire world. In 1902 an office was opened in New York. Stanley Gibbons died in 1913.

Stanley Gibbons' headquarters are now at 399 Strand – the world's largest stamp shop – and there are also offices in Melbourne and Singapore. The company continues to trade at all levels of philately, from rare stamps to stamp collecting starter packs for children.

ELIDA GIBBS

After the Norman Conquest of 1066, a man named de Guibbe, who had accompanied William the Conqueror to England, moved to Scotland. The family became bonnet makers in Paisley, until the industry fell on hard times when they turned their talent to the trade of 'Maltsters, Fleshing and Tallow Chandlers'. This was their first association with soap making, and a family business was established in 1712.

In 1768, Alexander Gibb opened a factory in Clerkenwell in London. This is the first reference to the name of Gibbs being spelt in this form. Alexander's son, David, carried on the business, eventually passing it into the hands of David and William, whose initials were incorporated into the name of the company, D & W Gibbs Ltd.

The house of Gibbs is therefore one of the oldest, if not the oldest, soap houses in the country. Its early chief interest was in candles, but soap gradually came to play a more important part. By the early years of the nineteenth century the major part of the business was in hard soap, toilet soaps and shaving soaps. Considerable

business had been built up in France by an agent, mainly for shaving soap and cold cream soap. In 1906 he asked Gibbs to produce a solid dentifrice for the French market. At that time the chief dentifrices were in the form of powders, although tooth soap had a small market. The solid dentifrice produced for the French market was in effect the modern toothpaste in a solid form. This new form of tooth-cleaning product was marketed in this country under the name of 'Gibbs

French Dentifrice'. It became very popular with the British troops in France during the First World War.

When Gerard Gibbs came back from the war, he started an advertising campaign which put the company on the map as one of the major makers of dental products. In 1934, Gibbs SR was launched. It contained sodium ricinoleate, a gum health ingredient, from which the name SR is derived.

Signal was first launched in the United Kingdom in 1960 as Shield, along with the slogan, 'The toothpaste with the mouthwash in the stripes'. When fluoride was added it was renamed Signal 2.

From 1917 and 1940

His Favourite

A Soldier writes from Salonica:

"Tommy prefers Gibbs's Dentifrice because of its economy in use, the fresh and clean sensation it imparts to the mouth; it keeps the teeth sound and of good colour, and, moreover, being a solid cake, can be stowed away in the haversack without risk of damage to other contents. I have seen fellows' haversacks in a terrible mess through a tooth-paste tube having burst, or powder tin falling open."

Send a tin of Gibbs's—the delicious French Dentifrice—in your next parcel, and use Gibbs's yourself. You will like it.

"Like a breeze in the Mouth."

Price 6d.   -   -   Of all Chemists.

Gibbs's Dentifrice

GENEROUS TRIAL SAMPLES of Shaving Soap, Dentifrice, and Cold Cream Soap sent on receipt of 2d. in stamps.

D & W. GIBBS, Ltd. (Dept. 22H), Cold Cream Soap Works, London, E. 1.   Est. 1712.

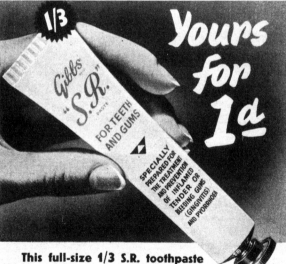

This full-size 1/3 S.R. toothpaste for 1d. and two empty 6d. S.R. cartons

This generous offer helps you to save your money *and* your teeth. All you have to do to get a 1/3 tube of Gibbs S.R. is collect two empty 6d. S.R. cartons and hand them, with one penny, to your chemist! Gibbs S.R., because it contains Sodium Ricinoleate, the dentist's own treatment for gum diseases, prevents and cures pyorrhoea and gingivitis, the diseases which undermine the teeth. Use Gibbs S.R. regularly for healthy gums and sound teeth.

GIBBS

S.R.

TOOTHPASTE

THIS OFFER DOES NOT APPLY IN EIRE

GR 84-14   D. & W. GIBBS LTD., LONDON, E.I

Gillette

King Camp Gillette was born in 1855 in Fond du Lac, Wisconsin, but a few years later moved to live in Chicago. His father and three brothers were all inventors, each holding a number of US patents.

As a teenager, King had tried inventing but with little success, and when he was seventeen years old he started work as a travelling salesman. In 1891 he began work at the Baltimore Seal Co, where he met William Painter, the inventor of the crown cork. Painter urged Gillette to concentrate his inventiveness on a product that could be purchased over and over again.

The idea intrigued Gillette, and he would go through the alphabet considering all the things people used frequently, hoping to find inspiration. Then one morning in 1895 at his home in Brookline, Massachusetts he started to shave – but the blade of his razor was so dull he could not use it, and it would need professional sharpening. Suddenly the idea of a new razor and blade flashed through his mind. He quickly saw a sequence of parts: a very thin piece of steel with an edge on both sides, a handle, and a clamp to centre the blade over the handle. He was certain that this product – one that would be purchased over and over again – was the great invention he was looking for.

Gillette's faith in his idea was to be severely tested over the coming months and years. He worked hard to perfect the new razor but the idea became a standing joke among his friends. Others to whom he went for help advised him to drop the idea as being highly impractical.

In 1901 a mutual friend outlined Gillette's safety razor idea to William Nickerson, who reluctantly agreed to study the idea more closely. Nickerson estimated that they would need $5,000 to manufacture the razor on a commercial scale. While Gillette started trying to sell stock in the 'American Safety Razor Company', Nickerson began creating machinery in a friend's shop on Atlantic Avenue in Boston.

King Camp Gillette

His first attempts at grinding and hardening produced crooked, crumpled blades, but he created machines and processes that were as novel as the safety razor itself. While manufacturing progress continued, financing for the company, now named the Gillette Safety Razor Company, was still uncertain. The few stock-holders Gillette had managed to get were becoming impatient.

Production finally started in 1903. That year they sold 51 razor sets and 168 blades. 1904 was more encouraging. By the end of 1905, production had grown to 250,000 razor sets and nearly 100,000 blade packages, each containing a dozen blades. 1906 saw the payment of the first dividend.

During the next ten years, blade sales rocketed to 7,000,000 a year, whilst sets continued to sell at between 300,000 – 400,000 per year. The outer wrapper of these blades and razors carried the name and face of King Camp Gillette as the company trademark.

In 1917 the American Government placed an order for 3^1/$_2$ million razors and 36 million blades – enough to supply the entire armed forces!

In 1923 the company introduced a gold-plated razor at $l each. They also conceived a new sales approach – with each box of Wrigley's Gum a dealer purchased, they received a free razor set. More than one million

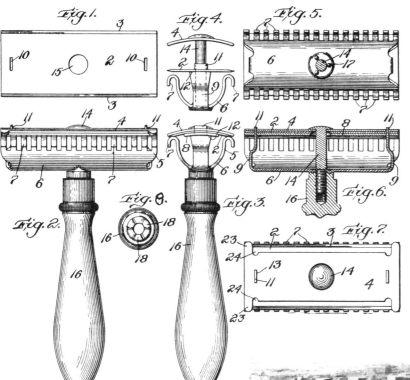

No. 775,134.

PATENTED NOV. 15, 1904.

K. C. GILLETTE.
RAZOR.
APPLICATION FILED DEC. 3, 1901.

NO MODEL.

Silver Brownie razor sets were supplied in this promotion.

Today the company has diversified into toiletries and cosmetics, stationery products, electric shavers and domestic appliances, and dental care products. They sell over 900 products in over 200 nations and territories.

The Gillette Safety Razor Co factory in Boston

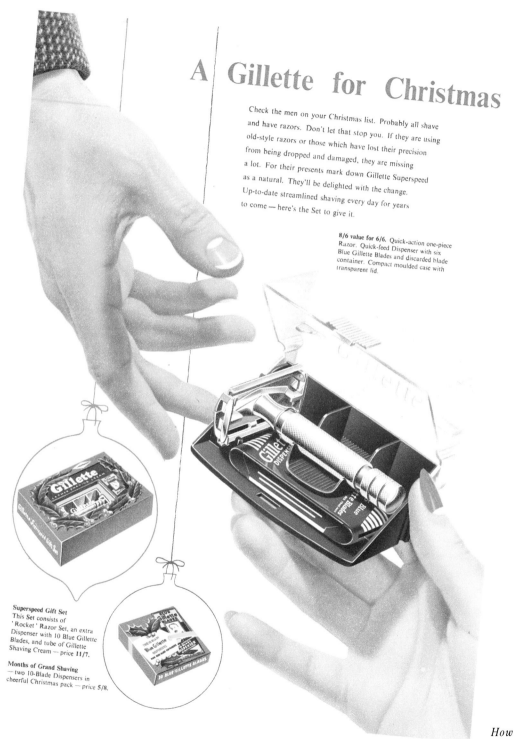

A Gillette for Christmas

Check the men on your Christmas list. Probably all shave and have razors. Don't let that stop you. If they are using old-style razors or those which have lost their precision from being dropped and damaged, they are missing a lot. For their presents mark down Gillette Superspeed as a natural. They'll be delighted with the change. Up-to-date streamlined shaving every day for years to come — here's the Set to give it.

8/6 value for 6/6. Quick-action one-piece Razor. Quick-feed Dispenser with six Blue Gillette Blades and discarded blade container. Compact moulded case with transparent lid.

The ideal Christmas gift in 1954

Superspeed Gift Set
This Set consists of 'Rocket' Razor Set, an extra Dispenser with 10 Blue Gillette Blades, and tube of Gillette Shaving Cream — price 11/7.

Months of Grand Shaving
— two 10-Blade Dispensers in cheerful Christmas pack — price 5/8.

In the late 1890s, several inventors started experimenting with the idea of a machine that could suck up dust and dirt. In 1900, Hubert Cecil Booth attended a demonstration at St Pancras Station in London which was to show how much cleaner railway carriages would be if you could blow the dirt from one side of the carriage into a dustbox on the other side. Unfortunately the dust did not oblige, but Mr Booth left the station thinking about the problem.

Hubert Cecil Booth. A very versatile man, he designed and supervised the erection of the Great Wheels at Blackpool, Paris and Vienna – the latter still operating

On returning home, he wetted a piece of cloth, placed it over the arm of a chair, and used his lungs like a pair of bellows to suck air through the cloth. The result was a visible patch of dirt on the cloth. In Mr Booth's own words, he had invented the 'vacuum cleaner'.

Mr Booth patented his invention in 1901. He formed the 'Vacuum Cleaner Co Ltd' to manufacture and sell the invention. The first cleaner was rather expensive at £350! This bright red machine with its five horse-power piston engine measured 4ft 6ins by 4ft 10ins by 3ft 6ins. When you wanted your home cleaned, it arrived on a horsedrawn cart with a team of men in white drill suits!

While Westminster Abbey was being prepared for the coronation of King Edward VII and Queen Alexandra, Mr Booth was invited to prove the cleaning powers of his new invention on the coronation carpet. The royal household was very impressed, and the king and queen requested Mr Booth to do a further demonstration in their presence at Buckingham Palace. His demonstration was so successful that his first two machines were sold to Buckingham Palace and Windsor Castle. Later the company was given the Royal Warrant of Appointment to His Majesty.

In 1903 he was granted world patent

The police took a very dim view of Booth's first vacuum cleaner – which had to stay in the street – and fined the company for obstruction. Eventually a test case was taken to appeal, and the Lord Chief Justice upheld their right to work from the streets

Goblin's first Teasmade included two earthenware cups, saucers, cream jug and sugar basin

rights for the vacuum cleaner. This started a long round of legal battles, but he won his actions. The company was now going all out for sales and soon had orders for fixed cleaning machines at the Houses of Parliament, Savoy Hotel, Gaiety Theatre and many other important buildings, both in London and the provinces.

In 1904 he produced the world's first portable vacuum cleaner, although it needed two people to operate it, one pumping the bellows, the other operating the cleaning tool. (At that time very few houses had electricity.) Even the Royal Mint wanted a demonstration and this was done. However, as the van returned with its mobile power unit the police stopped it and escorted it back to the Mint. They had inadvertently managed to walk out with the dustbag containing a fair amount of gold dust!

The company's first upright bag model was produced in 1921. The first cylindrical model, called the Turbinet, was produced a few years later. Subsequently it was decided to put the whole range of domestic cleaners under the trade name of 'Goblin'. It is said that the managing director's wife said of the cleaner that it was 'goblin up the dirt', and so the name was born.

The other product for which Goblin is well known is the 'Teasmade'. The development of tea-making machines started long before Goblin came on the scene. In 1891 a man named Rowbottom patented one, and not long afterwards a Birmingham gunsmith, Frank Smith, produced one operated by a spring-wound alarm clock.

The first Goblin Teasmade was invented by Brenner Thornton in 1936. He used electricity to power his automatic teamaker, far the safest method. Goblin bought his invention the following year and it sold very successfully for £5 15s 6d. Thoughout

the years, Goblin have kept the styling of the Teasmade up to date but there has been no need to change the working mechanism.

In 1984 the Goblin brand name and range of vacuum cleaners were acquired by Shop-Vac, who developed domestic wet/dry vacuum cleaning under the AquaVac brand in the UK and Europe.

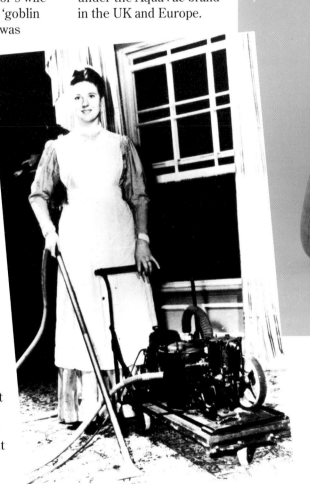

The BVC Non-Electric (above) *was produced in 1908 for the first Ideal Home Exhibition. Two people were required to operate it – one to turn the wheel and one to do the cleaning. However, this was not a problem, as Edwardian customers who could afford a vacuum cleaner also had maid servants!*

This 1927 model (left) *was more portable*

Gossard

Around the turn of the present century, Henry Williamson Gossard was producing foundation wear for ladies in Chicago. They were very different garments from the ones we know today, but twice a year he made the long trip from America to Paris to purchase the beautiful French silks and brocades. From these materials he fashioned his high-class range of 'hidden garments'.

In 1900, Gossard was on one of his visits to Paris and went to the theatre to see the famous actress Sarah Bernhardt in the role of Napoleon II, a twenty-one year old dying consumptive. In her younger days she had been well-known for performances like *Hamlet* in London's West End, but at the age of fifty-six she no longer had the sylph-like figure of her youth! Gossard was fascinated with the under-garment which enabled the middle-aged actress to successfully portray this dying youth. Sensing the potential impact of the corset, he returned to America with the secret of its construction, and in 1901 founded the H W Gossard Company, bringing a new concept in foundation garments.

In 1921 the H W Gossard Company opened a London office in Regent Street. Their first sales catalogue offered corsets and brassieres for all types of figure – the fabrics included silks, satins, brocades, cottons, surgical or hand knitted elastic, suede and even a material called granite cloth!

In 1925, Gossard was promoting a type of corselette known as 'The Gossard Complete' – 'On in 17 seconds' – and a rubber reducing corselette designed to give a 'decidedly flat back'. At about this time, Gossard took the revolutionary step of moving the lacing from the back to the front of a corset, making hundreds of ladies' maids redundant overnight – they were no longer needed to fasten up their mistresses' corsets! Not only that, but the new garments were also more comfortable to wear. They immediately sold in enormous quantities.

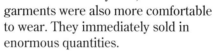

H W Gossard in 1916

The early bras were often known as 'bust bodices'. They could be best described as bust improvers – generally they were shapeless garments in cotton cambric, or for the very rich, loose-fitting camisole tops were available in beautiful lace.

Even in the 1920s, no bras were available of the types we know today. The 'Flappers' – the trendy young girls of the 1920s – actually went to great lengths to flatten the bust. It was really not until the 1930s that we start to see the move towards present-day fashions.

However a little before that, in 1926, Gossard opened their first UK factory, having been exporting to this country for many years. During the war years, much of the work there was in making parachutes and rubber dinghies for the RAF. But once the war was over, new lighter garments became fashionable, using such new materials as elastic rubber nets and nylon. In 1959, Gossard became part of the Courtauld Group.

In the early 1960s, Gossard pioneered the pantie girdle and the bra-slip, both thought to be very daring at the time. However the later 1960s were more difficult days, with the development of tights, which led to many younger women discarding the roll-ons and suspenders. In 1968, Gossard advertised a new girdle, and for decency also showed the model wearing a lacy low-cut bra. The general reaction was: 'Forget the girdle, where can I get the bra'. It was the Gossard Wonderbra, and it has continued to be a bestseller for over twenty years. After the bra-burning era, in 1977 they introduced sheer, shimmering bras and briefs – they also made them in a wider range of cup fittings to meet the changing figures of young women. Today the move is towards colour and fabric co-ordinated lingerie in a wide range of fittings

Gossard is an international company, also incorporating the Berlei range of garments, exporting to countries as diverse as Iceland and Australia, with needs as various as for D cups in Deutschland and A cups in Asia!

The early Gossard corset

The Wonderbra

Henry Heinz was born in 1844, and when he was five years old his family moved to Sharpsburgh near Pittsburgh.

When only sixteen years old he began to dry and grate horseradish and sell it in glass bottles. Unlike others of his time, he packed his horseradish in clear bottles, which meant that his customers could see for themselves that it was only horseradish, without added bits of turnip or other foreign matter. His claims for his products – no artificial preservatives, no impurities, no colouring matter, plus a

The first tins of baked beans had a piece of pork in – but Heinz still catered for every taste

reckless money-back guarantee if they failed to please – were unheard of then. Even today his principles still govern the company he founded, and are spelled out on every Heinz can or bottle label.

In the early 1870s, along with a friend, L C Noble, they had formed Heinz Noble and Company, selling their 'Anchor Brand' products. Soon they were cultivating 160 acres and employing 150 people in the peak season. However, in 1875 the depression which had hit America two years earlier also affected them and forced the company into voluntary liquidation. Henry listed his moral obligations as to repay all his creditors in full – he achieved it by 1884.

In 1876 he persuaded his brother, John, and cousin, Frederick, to put up enough money to get the F & J Heinz Company launched, with Henry as their salaried manager.

In June 1886, Henry J Heinz made his famous visit to Europe, calling at Fortnum & Mason, London's most illustrious grocery store and purveyor to the queen. The forty-two year old salesman, complete with top hat, frock

coat and bristling energy, asked for the head of grocery purchasing. He produced 'seven varieties of our finest and newest goods' which he had brought with him. The head of grocery purchasing tasted, considered and gave the famous reply:

'I think, Mr Heinz, we will take the lot.'

Henry Heinz at the time of his first London visit

As we have seen, Henry Heinz was a man of strong principle, gained from his Lutheran parents. On his first day in London, a Sunday, he took his family to Wesley's Chapel in City Road for morning service – he sat at Charles Wesley's reading desk and in John Wesley's chair ('I felt I was on holy ground'). In later years, his support of religious causes – particularly the world Sunday school movement – was to become his great passion.

By 1888 he had bought out John and Frederick, and restyled the enterprise H J Heinz Company. It was the founder who hit on the idea of the slogan '57 varieties'. He spotted an advert while riding on the New York elevated train which said: '21 Styles of Shoes'. Henry Heinz started to count his own products, which even then exceeded 60. But the number 57 appealed to him – 'The idea gripped me at once' he said – and the slogan has stayed the same ever since. Today

From a hansom cab — to 'D' Day

IN JUNE 1886, a hansom cab drew up outside Fortnum & Mason's famous shop in Piccadilly. From it alighted a man of forty-two. He had with him five cases of goods. Shortly afterwards he hailed another hansom—without the five cases. For Fortnum & Mason had decided to take them all.

Thus, Mr. H. J. Heinz himself first introduced his now famous products to England.

In June 1944, included in the equipment of the Allied troops who stormed the Normandy beaches, were self-heating cans of soup — Heinz Soups. The flameless and smokeless heating element was lit with a match—or even a cigarette—and in a few minutes the contents of the can were piping hot. It had taken many years of experiment, in collaboration with Imperial Chemical

Industries Ltd., to perfect the self-heating can. Not until 1941 was success finally achieved.

The cases of 1886 and the cans of 1944 were identical in one respect — the quality of their contents.

For right from his early days when he first bottled and sold horseradish

from his mother's garden, Mr. Heinz was determined to build his business on one fundamental principle:

To make a thing that the world needs, to make it the best that it can be made, to get it into the hands of the largest number of people at a fair price, and to charge a reasonable fee for the service.

That principle, faithfully adhered to by successive generations, has carried the 57 Varieties to the four corners of the earth and has made the name of Heinz respected for quality everywhere.

That is the principle—the ideal—which we of the House of Heinz have never ceased to strive to uphold with all our might.

H. J. HEINZ COMPANY LIMITED, LONDON, N.W. 10

THE BRITISH HOUSE OF **HEINZ**

there are more than 1,200 products worldwide.

The first canned beans were made by Burnham and Morrill in 1875 and were flavoured with pork and molasses. In 1895, Heinz produced their first batch of baked beans with tomato sauce. The original product contained a piece of pork, but this was deleted from the recipe in the 1940s due to wartime shortages, and has never been replaced. Baked beans were introduced into the United Kingdom in the early 1900s, although they were not manufactured in England until 1928.

Cream of tomato soup was introduced in 1910 from Pittsburgh – today nine million cans of this soup are sold each day in Britain.

With the headquarters still in Pittsburgh, USA, H J Heinz Company distributes products all over the world.

Above   *Labelling of all Heinz baked beans was originally done by hand*

Right   *This became a national catchphrase*

Mr W H 'Boss' Hoover and his son, Mr H W Hoover, were successful harness and leather goods manufacturers.

A local inventor, Mr J Murray Spangler, brought a model of his 'electric suction sweeper' to them; it was a crude machine, made of tin and wood with a broom handle. The Hoovers were looking around for other possible enterprises, and 'Boss' Hoover saw the potentialities of the cleaner. In 1908 he began its manufacture and sales promotion.

With the growing popularity of the Hoover cleaner, the business was turned over entirely to the manufacture of domestic appliances after the end of the First World War.

The first Hoover factory outside the United States was in Canada, and it was from there that the first Hoover cleaners were shipped to Britain. In 1919 Hoover Ltd was registered in London, building the first British Hoover factory at Perivale, Middlesex in 1932.

Following the Second World War there was a renewed demand for Hoover cleaners. The company also started to extend its range of products, introducing the Hoover washing machine in 1948. At that time only 4% of homes in the United Kingdom were equipped with washing machines. Today this figure is about 89%.

The Hoover name is jealously protected as a trademark by Hoover plc.

Above
An early Hoover washing machine

Left
The Hoover Model 700 from 1926

Horlicks

James and William Horlick were born in the 1840s at Ruardean in the Forest of Dean. In 1869 William was persuaded to go to the United States by Joseph Horlick, a distant relative from Racine, Wisconsin.

Meanwhile, back in England, his brother had qualified as a pharmacist. In Germany, Liebig had experimented with vacuum drying and the concentration of food products. In America,

Gail Borden had recorded his patent in 1855 for the evaporation of condensed milk. These technological developments were of particular interest to the young chemist. James had himself experimented with the evaporation of malt food over a water bath and had subjected it to a vacuum in a flask, an adapted coffee pot. However, future prospects in England did not seem good. In 1873, James and his wife left for America to join William for a while.

When James could not find a partner, William finally decided to join him in

the manufacture of his artificial infant food, and the firm of J & W Horlick of Chicago was formed in late 1873. James started canvassing the medical profession and pharmaceutical trade, whereas William concentrated on the production side, book-keeping and financial matters.

In 1875, demand for the product had grown to a point where additional manufacturing space and warehouse facilities were required. William owned some land at Racine, and it was decided to build a factory there.

In 1883 they registered the patent for 'malted milk'. Under this process the 'wort', or extract prepared from a 'mash' of malted barley and wheat flour, was mixed with fresh whole milk, this being evaporated to dryness under vacuum. The resultant product, in powder form, could be mixed with hot water to give a beverage suitable for consumption by invalids and infants.

It later became necessary to build a much larger factory and warehouse, and in 1885 the 'Horlicks Food Company' was incorporated in the state of Wisconsin.

Part of the successful 1950s campaign –
(Thinks) '. . . *thanks to Horlicks!'*

Horlicks

MALTED FOOD DRINK

— FREE FROM ARTIFICIAL ADDITIVES —

Some time after 1890, James returned to England and established an office at Snow Hill, Holborn, London in 1894. The factory at Slough was built between 1906–1908. The first order in London was taken by James Horlick to supply Fortnum & Mason, the well-known grocers of Piccadilly.

Horlicks Malted Milk was supplied to the Arctic explorers, such as Amundsen, Evans, Scott and Shackleton. Up to the outbreak of the First World War the business went from strength to strength, and during that period the armed forces were supplied with Horlicks Malted Milk as emergency rations. In 1926 it was decided that William should keep the American business as his share, and that James' two sons, who had survived him, should have the English company and some cash. Each was to be run independently, but exchange information.

During 1931–33 the product was restyled as 'Horlicks', the words 'malted milk' being dropped from advertisements. Also at this time the highly successful phrase 'Night Starvation' was created. It was thought that a drink of Horlicks just before bedtime would maintain blood sugar levels and so give a restful sleep. Horlicks created a whole advertising campaign around this so-called 'Night Starvation'.

Years later, a similar campaign was launched featuring people whose happiness was threatened by lack of sleep. Horlicks is recommended to them, and their normal sleep returns, '. . . thanks to Horlicks'.

In 1945, Horlicks Milk Corporation (USA) was acquired by the English company. In India in 1960, a factory was started where buffalo rather than cow's milk was used. A further factory also exists in America.

The company is now part of the SmithKline Beecham Group, having been purchased in 1969 for approximately £20 million.

A 1925 advert

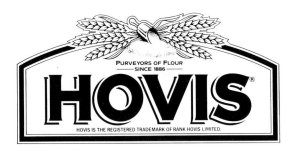

Richard Smith was born into a milling family at Stone, in Staffordshire. He conceived the idea of lightly cooking the vitamin-rich wheatgerm in steam so as to conserve its nourishing qualities, and then putting back into flour many times more wheatgerm than it would ordinarily contain.

Richard Smith patented his process in 1887. The finished product became known as 'Smith's Patent Germ Flour'

and was marketed by S Fitton & Son Ltd, millers of Macclesfield. Fittons organised a national competition to find a new name for their increasingly popular bread, and the word 'Hovis' was the invention of a Mr Herbert Grimes, a London student. He constructed it from the Latin phrase *hominis vis*, 'the strength of man'. Subsequently, Hovis bread first appeared in the shops in 1890.

Richard Smith died in 1900 and is buried in Highgate Cemetery, London, close to the grave of Karl Marx. His discovery of the Hovis process is recorded on his gravestone.

Hovis flour quickly became very popular with bakers and the name caught the public imagination. In 1898, Fitton & Son duly became the Hovis Bread Flour Company Limited and later established new flour mills in Manchester, Battersea and Lincoln. In 1918 the Hovis Bread Flour Company became Hovis Limited.

After the Second World War, Hovis Ltd merged with fellow millers McDougall Trust Ltd in 1957, and then with

1895

Joseph Rank Ltd in 1962 to become Rank Hovis McDougall Ltd.

Hovis have never baked a loaf of bread, but they have always ensured the quality of the bread baked from their flours. The tins for baking the bread still bear the Hovis name and must still be bought from the company, just as they were when Hovis began selling their patented flour.

Richard Smith, a miller, thought of lightly cooking the wheatgerm to preserve its goodness – and so made Hovis possible

Edwin Samson Moore worked as a representative for a pickle manufacturer and for a vinegar company. He had been born in 1849 and now, at the age of twenty-five, lived in Hockley Hill, Birmingham. He had a burning desire to set up his own vinegar brewery, and had seen some land for sale in Aston, Birmingham. Early in 1875 the Midland Vinegar Company was registered and, much to his wife's disgust, they moved to live next door to his brewery.

The site was an ideal one with plenty of possibility for expansion, and most importantly good 'hard' water from a well. In those days, vinegar brewing was an exacting task where crushed

A memorandum heading from 1906, showing the sauce works

barley, with malt, was mixed with water then heated almost to boiling. The resultant liquid, known as the wort, was then tested until it was of the right gravity for producing the correct strength of vinegar. After several further processes, a 'starter' of vinegar was added. The vinegar then had to mature.

The return of English families towards the end of the century from the outposts of the Empire popularised spiced recipes. Samson had no doubt that the time was ripe for the introduction of a new sauce. He felt, however, that the sauce must have a catchy name; the right name was half the battle. One day he set off to see Mr F G Garton of Nottingham, one of his vinegar debtors. He, and his son Eddie who was now an important part of the firm, were shown into a back room where a sauce was cooking in the wash-house copper.

However it was the basket-cart standing in the yard that caught Samson's eye. On it was crudely painted the words 'Garton's H. P. Sauce' – that was the name he wanted! In a few minutes a deal was struck, Mr Garton's debt was cancelled and a further £150 was paid for the name and the recipe.

HP Sauce had to be sold at a price poor families could afford. The first cheap daily morning paper, the *Daily Mail*, had been an instant success among the working class – Samson and Eddie made sure their advertisements could be read by the families.

Following the turn of the century, a nationwide advertising campaign was launched and door-to-door salesmen sold miniature bottles of HP Sauce. The expenditure was large, but once Samson felt that his products were selling themselves he would spend no more on advertising. Mr Garton had tentatively claimed that his sauce was used in the restaurants of the Houses of Parliament; Samson knew for a fact that it was available there and had heard it rumoured that it was also used at 10 Downing Street.

Edwin Samson Moore in 1890

Overseas sales were also going well, with products going to Canada, Sweden, Denmark, France, South Africa, Australia and New Zealand. The range of products now also included custard and baking powders, lemonade crystals and lime juice cordial, jelly crystals, coffee essence and gravy browning.

Another new sauce was about to be launched in 1912 – Daddie's Favourite – to fill the gap in the market for a cheaper sauce. However, the production of the sauces was kept separate, the works girls being nicknamed Daddie's Girls, the others the HP Snobs!

As the years rolled by, Samson realised that his health was failing and that Eddie's children did not want to come into the business. Now was the time to sell, and on 31st December 1924, HP Sauce Ltd was floated by the British Shareholders' Trust.

Lea and Perrins of Worcester was acquired in 1930.

In 1967 the company became a wholly owned subsidiary of the Imperial Tobacco Company, later to become Imperial Foods Ltd.

One of the original bottle labels printed in French in 1917. The firm held many government contracts in the First World War, and the troops maintained that their sauces made 'bully beef' palatable. When the description in French was later withdrawn, letters of complaint were sent to The Times

JACOBS

The Jacob family originated in south-west England, but having adopted the Quaker faith, Richard Jacob decided, in 1675, to move with his family to Southern Ireland, having suffered much religious persecution.

Richard's great-great grandson died in 1839, leaving two very young sons and a thriving business making bread and sea biscuits, and also a barm (yeast) brewery which supplied Waterford, in those days a port of considerable importance. William and his younger brother Robert formed a partnership, W & R Jacob, continuing the business. Tragically Robert was drowned in 1861.

In 1850, William had the idea of starting to manufacture 'fancy' biscuits. The following advertisement appeared in the *Waterford Mail*:

> Having commenced the manufacture of fancy biscuits, we hope to secure for our Waterford made Biscuits a portion of the present demand for those imported from Carlisle and Edinburgh.
>
> W. & R. JACOB
>
> Bridge Street,
> November 6th, 1850

At the time of the advertisement, William little thought that in his day he would see the biscuits being 'exported' to, and sold in, Carlisle and Edinburgh (and that eventually they would also be sold as far away as Vancouver and Hong Kong). So interested was he in the idea, he paid a visit to England in 1851 to study the trade and with a view to commencing manufacturing them in England himself. On his way back he passed through Dublin, noticing a large vacant coach factory in Peter's Row. He purchased the lease of the premises and moved the business from Waterford to Dublin. Following the death of Robert, William Frederick Bewley joined the company as a partner; it strengthened a family link back to Waterford and has continued to the present day.

In 1883, William's son George visited America and saw the American soda cracker. As a result of this, experiments were carried out back in Dublin, and the following year the cream cracker was perfected and launched. The dough used in biscuit making is normally ready for baking within twenty minutes of being made, but with the fermented dough used in cream crackers, this may take up to twenty-four hours.

W. & R. JACOB & Co., LTD.
Biscuit & Cake Manufacturers. DUBLIN.
Established 1851.
BY APPOINTMENT

- GENERAL VIEW OF FACTORY, DUBLIN -
WAREHOUSES & OFFICES AT LONDON, LIVERPOOL & MANCHESTER.

Cream crackers quickly became a best seller and its sales have continued to grow ever since. In 1886, Albert Jacob came to England and built up the business in Britain, opening a factory in Liverpool in 1914. Following the creation of the Irish Free State in 1922, the English and Irish companies were separated.

In 1928, another major step forward was taken by the development of the use of airtight cartons for biscuits.

Today the British company has its headquarters at Reading, and is very much involved in producing biscuits for the home market as well as exporting to many parts of the world.

In Ireland, Jacobs acquired the biscuit interests of Bolands and formed Irish Biscuits Ltd, a company which also has extensive export interests. Today they produce over a hundred different products, baking no less than 12 million biscuits a day!

Johnson & Johnson

The Johnson brothers, Robert Wood Johnson, James Wood Johnson and Edward Mead Johnson, formed a partnership in 1885, and operations began in New Brunswick, New Jersey, USA a year later. It had fourteen employees and was based on the fourth floor of a small building that was once a wallpaper factory. In 1887 the company was incorporated as Johnson & Johnson. Johnson & Johnson had entered the surgical dressings industry.

Robert Wood Johnson was a pioneer of sterile surgical dressings

Sir Joseph Lister, the noted English surgeon, had at that time identified airborne germs as a source of infection in the operating room. Whilst many people were contemptuous of Lister's work, Robert Wood Johnson, who had heard him speak, had no such misgivings and had it in his mind to create a ready-made, sterile, wrapped and sealed surgical dressing.

The first products were improved medicinal plasters containing medical compounds mixed in an adhesive. Soon this was followed by a soft, absorbent cotton and gauze dressing that could be mass-produced and shipped in quantity to hospitals, physicians and drugstores.

By 1890 they were treating cotton and gauze dressings by dry heat in an attempt to produce not only an antiseptic product, but also a sterile one. It was in the same year that they also introduced the famous Johnson's Baby Powder. A physician wrote to the company saying one of his patients was complaining of skin irritation from using a medicated plaster. In response they sent the patient a small tin of Italian talc, and from then on a small can of talc was included with some packs of plasters. Soon customers asked for more of the powder, leading to the birth of a product which invariably reminds users of happy thoughts of childhood.

The Johnsons corresponded regularly with the originators of a new product called Coca-Cola, which was introduced in Atlanta in 1886. In 1894 Johnson & Johnson introduced the first of their 'kola' preparations, which was recommended for the relief of nausea, to regulate the pulse, and increase stamina and endurance. It was also supposed to sober drunks!

In 1920 another of Johnson & Johnson's famous products, the Band-Aid adhesive bandage, was 'discovered' quite by accident. Earle E Dickson, a cotton mill employee, was distressed because his young bride, Josephine, was constantly cutting herself while working in the kitchen. Patiently Dickson bandaged her fingers, but the accidents kept occurring. Finally he decided to make a ready-to-use bandage that she could apply herself. Laying out a long strip of surgical tape, he placed small pieces of gauze on it at regular intervals, and to keep the adhesive from sticking he covered it with pieces of textured cotton or crinoline. Whenever Josephine wounded herself, she cut a piece of the tape and gauze pad and used it as a bandage.

Today Johnson & Johnson are not only widely known for their Baby Powder (and its close relations such as baby soap and baby oil) and Band Aid, but for a vast range of products specially designed to meet the needs of the world's professionals in health care. These include the manufacture of disposable surgical packs and gowns, surgical sutures, pain relieving products, and a wide range of products for dermatology and dental care. Worldwide the company employs more than 83,000 people in the family of 175 companies spread throughout 52 countries.

In 1886, Samuel Curtis Johnson bought a parquet flooring business in Racine, Wisconsin, USA. People liked his new floors, but the cleaning methods which were then available ruined the surface. However, he understood about such surfaces for he had been a carpenter. He was asked to

Samuel Curtis Johnson (left) *started the business, and his son Herbert Fisk Johnson opened the first London office*

prepare a wax paste suitable for such floors and soon realised that there was a need for more cleaning products for furniture, shoes and for new automobiles.

In 1914, as Europe was stumbling towards war, Samuel's son, Herbert Fisk Johnson, arrived in Britain and opened a small office in London. The first consignment of wax from Racine never reached England as a German torpedo sent it to the sea bed. But it needed more than this to deter Herbert Johnson. Within a couple of years it became necessary to move to

larger premises – Colham Mill in West Drayton, Middlesex.

In 1922 the import of goods from Racine gradually ceased and manufacturing began at West Drayton. By 1923 the whole of the United Kingdom's needs were produced in England. During this same decade they made their first faltering steps into radio advertising, then a novelty in the United Kingdom.

The future was looking bright, but then came the outbreak of the Second World War. It was, however, during this difficult period that the first export from England took place – ski wax was shipped to the Soviet Union to help speed the Red Army over the snow during the siege of Leningrad.

After the war, several new products were introduced, among them a furniture polish, Pledge, which was to become a market leader. Such was the growth of the company that in 1960 a sixty-six acre site was developed at Frimley Green in Surrey.

Today the company is still very much a family business. The chairman, Samuel C Johnson, is a

great-grandson of the founder. The range of products is ever increasing, and now includes air fresheners, insecticides, shampoos, and shaving foam – not, of course, forgetting polish.

A Polish and Protection *for* the Finest Finishes

JOHNSON'S PREPARED WAX

FINE finishes require proper care — whether they are on furniture, pianos, woodwork, doors or motor cars. A thin, glasslike coat of transparent wax, rubbed to a brilliant polish preserves and protects the original finish from dust, grime and dampness, adding years to its life.

A Dust-Proof Polish

Oily polishes gather and hold the dust, soiling clothing, linen, and everything with which they come in contact. **Johnson's Prepared Wax** imparts a perfectly hard, dry polish to which dust and dirt cannot adhere. It never becomes sticky or tacky in the hottest weather nor from the heat of the body—consequently does not show finger prints.

Motor Car Owners

You will find Johnson's Prepared Wax just the thing for polishing the body, bonnet and wings of your car. It sheds water and does not gather dust—makes a "wash" last twice as long.
There are many uses for Johnson's Prepared Wax. Try it for polishing your

Floors	Piano	Boots
Linoleum	Furniture	Saddlery
Woodwork	Leather Goods	Gun Stocks

Johnson's Prepared Wax is conveniently put up—always ready for use—no tools or brushes required—all you need is a cheese-cloth rag.

USE THE COUPON for Generous Sample Tins

Johnson's Cleaner

is just the thing for *old cars*—it *entirely* removes all stains, discolorations, scum, road-oil, tar and grease. Even those spots that you thought were permanent will disappear like magic under Johnson's Cleaner. And it doesn't injure or scratch the finest varnish —simply cleans it and prepares it for a coat of Johnson's Wax.

Johnson's Cleaner is also excellent for cleaning *old furniture* and *woodwork* before waxing—particularly good for *desks*.

S. C. JOHNSON & SON, 244 High Holborn, London, W. C.

I enclose 6d for a sample tin each of Johnson's Prepared Wax and Johnson's Cleaner, sufficient for cleaning and polishing several pieces of furniture, a large square of Linoleum or a large car.

Name...

Address..

Kellogg's

At Battle Creek, Michigan in America in 1866, the wife of the minister of the Seventh Day Adventist Church had the idea that a diet based on grains, nuts and foods of vegetable origin was essential to 'right living'. The Western Health Reform Institute was set up at Battle Creek, and in 1876 Dr John Harvey Kellogg was appointed chief physician. He became interested in developing an easy-to-digest breakfast to replace the rather heavy meal which was then widely taken.

With his brother William Keith, Dr Kellogg developed a paper-thin malt-flavoured toasted flake of maize, which proved so popular that he received many requests from ex-patients for regular supplies to be posted to them. Demand continued to grow between 1902–1904. In 1906, William Keith established the Battle Creek Toasted Corn Flake Company in a small wooden building in the town. After just one year it was destroyed by fire, but he was undeterred and built a larger and better plant.

He insisted on rigid quality controls, and attended to every detail of production. To avoid confusion with his many competitors, William Keith had his signature printed on each packet, and for many years they also bore the slogan: 'The original bears this signature'.

W K Kellogg was a hardworking business-man and marketing innovator

Kellogg advertised his product extensively, and production rose from an initial thirty-three cases per day to over one million by 1909. The advertising budget in 1911 was $1 million and the next year the world's biggest sign appeared in Times Square, New York, with a sixty-six foot high 'K' in the word 'Kellogg's'.

Kellogg's pioneered nutritional labelling in the 1930s, produced an increased-protein cereal, Special K, in

Three boxes from 1950

1955, and has been adding nutrients to their grains since the 1940s.

In 1986 there were 22 plants operating in 17 countries, and annual sales in more than 130 countries are now $6 billion.

Today the range extends to twenty different products, but still Corn Flakes are the most popular both here and throughout the world. The factory at Stretford, Manchester, produces around two million packets of cereal every day. Additionally they own the largest corn-mill in Europe at Seaforth, Liverpool – it processes 1,000 tons of grain per day.

The illustrations and the Kellogg's logo are reproduced by kind permission of the Kellogg Company   © Kellogg Company

There are some imaginative recipes in this 1954 advert

ROUND THE CLOCK WITH *Kellogg's*

First thing in the morning—Kellogg's Corn Flakes with your breakfast help to give you a good start to the day.

In a hurry for a lunch-time sweet? Try a block of ice-cream smothered in golden Corn Flakes and topped with a hot jam sauce. It's a winner every time!

Ever tried Corn Flakes and cold rice pudding with added condensed milk! It's a wonderful cold sweet for the TV interval, guaranteed not to upset delicate tummies.

Crisp, golden, crunchy Corn Flakes are heavenly to eat *any* time of day. Give the family a treat—let them enjoy their Kellogg's whenever the fancy takes them. Clever housewives can concoct lots more variations on this single, delicious theme.

ALL KELLOGG'S CEREALS ARE GOOD TO EAT— ANY TIME!

BRAN FLAKES

ALL-BRAN

RICE KRISPIES

CORN FLAKES

More people like Kellogg's most

Kodak

George Eastman was born in Waterville, New York, in 1854. When George was six years old the family moved to Rochester, and two years later his father died. Due to poverty, George then had to leave school at fourteen and he vowed he would relieve the family of their financial distress.

When he was twenty-four years old, he thought he needed a holiday and, having read about Santo Domingo, decided to go there. It was suggested he must make a photographic record of the trip. In the end he did not make the trip, but he did become fully absorbed in photography and wanted to simplify the complicated process.

On reading British magazines he discovered that photographers were making their own gelatine plates which remained sensitive after they were dry. This contrasted to the earlier wet plates which had to be exposed at once. Eastman began making gelatine plates for his own pleasure, and later for sale to others.

In 1880 he leased the third floor of a building in State Street in Rochester, and started to manufacture dry plates for sale. As difficulties were overcome, so he turned his attention to the development of new products which would simplify photography. At first he intended this to be for the benefit of professional photographers, but later realised that if his business was to really expand he would have to reach the general public.

With this in mind, he decided to make a new kind of camera. The first Kodak camera was introduced in June 1888. But why Kodak? George Eastman explained:

George Eastman, the father of modern photography

'I devised the name myself . . . The letter "K" had been a favourite with me – it seems a strong, incisive sort of letter . . . It became a question of trying out a great number of combinations of letters that made words, starting and ending with "K". The word Kodak was the result.'

The distinctive Kodak yellow, used for packaging their products, is widely known throughout the world and is one of the company's most valued assets.

The first Kodak camera was a box-type camera, light and small, loaded with a roll of stripping paper, long enough for 100 exposures. After exposure the camera was sent to Rochester, where the exposed strip was removed, developed and printed, and a new strip inserted. The camera had created an entirely new market, and made photographers of people who had no special knowledge of the subject, their only desire being to take pictures. Anybody could press the button and Mr Eastman's company would do the rest.

In the year 1889, Kodak introduced the first commercial roll film on transparent nitrocellulose support – this was the film which Thomas Edison used to make his motion pictures.

In 1891 the transparent film was further improved by spooling it so that it could be loaded into the camera in

A very early advert for the new Kodak cameras in 1889

The Folding Pocket Kodak – 'Prices from 26/- to 90/–' in 1904

daylight. No longer did the camera have to be sent to Rochester to be filled; rolls of film could be bought almost anywhere. Cameras for the new film were further simplified – a pocket-sized box camera was marketed in 1895. The Folding Pocket Kodak camera was fitted with bellows to make it collapsible.

In 1900 the first Brownie camera, intended for children, was put on the market at the price of $1. The Brownie was designed by Frank Brownell, but its name actually came from a character in American children's books which were very popular at the time. Early advertising was aimed almost entirely at children.

In 1928, experiments started in colour photography and, in 1935, Kodachrome film was introduced. In 1963, new excitement was stirred throughout the photographic world with the appearance of the Kodak Instamatic and four cartridge-loading films.

George Eastman was also a true philanthropist and dental clinics were particularly close to his heart and his giving. On one day in 1924 he signed away $30 million to three educational centres. He had sincere concern for negro education and two of these centres were concerned with this.

He died in 1932, having much enriched the world.

Colorsnap 35 camera. Just dial the weather on this precision 35 mm. camera to get colour pictures full of brilliant detail. Top quality 'Anaston' lens. £10.15.1d. Top Bantam Colorsnap camera. For fewer exposures at a loading—takes 'Kodachrome' film in 8 or 12-exposure rolls. £9.11.10d.

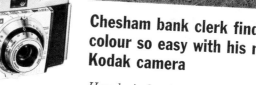

Snap to be proud of. Here is one of a fine set of pictures that John Edelsten took in Ireland with his Kodak 'Colorsnap' camera.

Chesham bank clerk finds colour so easy with his new Kodak camera

Here he is shooting his Irish holiday with his 'Colorsnap' camera

Bank clerk John Edelsten, of Chesham, and his wife Jean had never taken colour pictures before. But it seemed a grand idea for their holiday in Ireland. So they chose a Kodak 'Colorsnap' camera and loaded it with 'Kodachrome' film. Result, a wonderful set of colour pictures.

You, too, can get all the glowing colour of holidays and outings from the very first go, with a Kodak 'Colorsnap' camera.

You can take colour slides, colour prints and, of course, black-and-white pictures. Choose from two models of 'Colorsnap' cameras. See them at your Kodak dealer's today. Kodak films for the 'Colorsnap' cameras:— 'KODACHROME' film for colour slides 'KODACOLOR' film for colour prints And, of course, the famous Kodak black-and-white films.

Colour comes out best on

Kodak FILM

'Kodak' is a Registered Trade Mark

APRIL 1961—9

Ladybird Books Ltd

During the First World War a small firm of commercial printers in Loughborough, Wills and Hepworth, found they were not getting sufficient work to keep their machines and staff busy. William Simpson Hepworth felt that rather than continue to wait for more orders, and have an idle factory, they should produce something to sell. A decision was made to publish children's books and the name chosen was Ladybird. Alas no record was kept as to why the name was chosen.

The early Ladybird books bear no resemblance to those which we are so familiar with today, either in content or format. The books were larger and the illustrations were mainly black and white. However the books sold well and they served the purpose of providing business in the lean years of the war.

In 1939 they once again faced similar problems to those of the First World War, and once again they turned to children's books. By now they were more experienced as publishers and had better equipment. A careful investigation of the possibilities led to the standard format that is still the hallmark of Ladybird books. Each book has fifty-two pages, each page of text facing a full-page colour illustration.

The first new formula Ladybird books published in 1940 were stories of animals and nursery rhymes for very young children. In 1945, Wills and Hepworth continued as quality commercial printers and publishers – Ladybird books were too successful to be dropped. It was recognised that there was a good market for early information books, presented in the same colourful format that had been so successful for animal stories. The combination of these elements proved to be one of the most influential developments of modern times. The first of the new information books was published in the 1950s and proved an instant success. Today the books are used in schools and homes throughout the world. The 1960s saw the completion of the complete Ladybird Key Words Reading Scheme. The success of the scheme has been outstanding with sales exceeding 50 million books.

In the 1970s, Wills and Hepworth changed their name to the more appropriate one of Ladybird Books Limited. Recent years have seen phenomenal sales in both English editions and in over fifty other languages worldwide.

William Hepworth made the decision to publish children's books

This 1941 advert explains the new series

*A selection of books from the very first series
Ladybird published in their now world-famous
'pocket' format*

'Play-well'. Could you have a better name for a toy? Ole Kirk Christiansen created the name by putting the Danish words *leg godt* (play well) together.

He called his toy Lego. In Latin it means 'I am reading' or 'I am joining together', but he knew nothing about this.

In the 1930s, Ole Kirk Christiansen lost his job because of the depression in Denmark. At that time he was a carpenter in the tiny village of Billund on the moors of Jutland. He had an idea that he would create good toys which would appeal to children's imagination and their need to create, ones which would stand up to rough handling. His wooden toys became a success – yo-yos, elephants on wheels, and much more. Soon he was employing an increasing number of craftsmen.

By the end of the Second World War, some fifty people were employed by Lego and it had become the largest industry in the area; soon it was to grow larger still. His son, Gotfred, who had worked with him from the age of fourteen, travelled to England soon after the war, and on his way he discussed new ideas for toys with a toy dealer who was searching for a new kind of product, something with purpose, system and continuity.

Ideas came into his mind and he felt the answer lay in bricks which could

Wooden toys from the 1930s. The duck – the bestseller of its day – was marketed until production of wooden products stopped in 1960

be put together and then taken apart again. In 1955 in Denmark the now famous Lego brick was re-launched after much thought and experiment as a 'system of play'. The aim was that this new toy would appeal to boys and girls of all ages, be simple yet versatile, creative and aesthetically satisfying.

In 1958, Ole Kirk Christiansen died and the business was carried on by Gotfred. By this stage the annual turnover already exceeded £1 million and in the following year 90% of the production was for export.

In 1968, ten acres of heathland near the Lego factory were landscaped into a children's paradise called Legoland. It includes model villages, restaurants, dolls museums and many other attractions, Today over one million people come to Legoland each year.

In 1962 the toy became more versatile by introducing wheels to give Lego

cars; then the family of Lego figures was born; and in 1977 the Technical sets were created so working models could be made. Today Lego sets are exported to 106 countries and the leaflets printed in twenty-five different languages – 97% of the production at Billund is for export.

© Lego is a registered trade mark.

A JCB excavator from the new Lego Technic range

Part of the ten acre Legoland site

William Hesketh Lever, the son of a God-fearing wholesale grocer from Bolton, joined his father's firm when he was sixteen years old, becoming a partner five years later. By the time he was thirty-three years old he was already a wealthy man, but he had become disenchanted with the grocery business.

He had a great love of the Scottish islands, and whilst he was on holiday on one of them he made his decision to go into the soap trade – why soap, we do not know.

The household soap of that period was produced by a crude process of mixing tallow and remnants of raw alkali in large cauldrons; the resultant 'soap', which irritated the skin, was then made into bars, to be sliced into lengths by the grocer.

This early tablet is still preserved in the company's archives

The first thing Lever did was to consult an authority on trade marks. He wanted a name which was easy to remember, and easy to pronounce:

'Suddenly, I don't know how, after three or four days it flashed across me that Sunlight was the one . . . I was all of a tremble to have it registered, for fear someone else had got it.'

No-one else had got it, and on the 2nd February 1884 he registered the name.

He leased Winser's chemical works in Warrington, which made good soap but little money. The first experimental boil of Sunlight soap was on the 27th October 1885. The formula settled that day – a mix of coconut or palm kernel oil, cottonseed oil, resin and tallow – varied little until the twentieth century.

Orders cascaded in; he could barely satisfy the demand. To expand in the way he wanted, it was necessary to seek new land elsewhere. He found nothing in Lancashire, and so passing into Cheshire, he paused by a field gate and saw before him the land they were seeking. Today this land is only a few yards from the main entrance to the offices at Port Sunlight; the ground was then mostly marsh, being only a few feet above high water level and liable to be flooded by the Mersey tides. He knew what he required – good communications, ample and

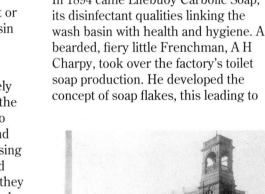

William Hesketh Lever was now Lord Leverhulme in 1901

cheap land, and a local labour force. Initially 56 acres was acquired, this being increased to 170 acres later.

After Mrs Lever cut the first sod, her husband announced that he would call the place Port Sunlight after the soap that was his lodestar.

By the middle of the 1890s they were selling nearly 40,000 tons of soap. He was already advertising his wares. He took out a contract for metal plate advertising with railway companies; this was only the start, as almanacs, booklets, diaries, and pamphlets on health were to follow.

In 1894 came Lifebuoy Carbolic Soap, its disinfectant qualities linking the wash basin with health and hygiene. A bearded, fiery little Frenchman, A H Charpy, took over the factory's toilet soap production. He developed the concept of soap flakes, this leading to

The imposing structure of the Number 1 Soapery, Port Sunlight, with its high tower which became a local landmark

How It All Began – Lever

the introduction of Sunlight Flakes, later to be called Lux. 1904 saw the introduction of Vim for household scouring.

At the end of the Boer War, Professor Glessier and Dr Bauer, both of Stuttgart, produced a soap with a bleaching agent. In 1909 the soap, now a powder, with a registered name of Persil, was bought by Crosfields, then a competitor of Lever Bros, from a German chemical firm. The name was derived from the roots, 'Per' and 'Sil', of the ingredients perborate and silicate. In 1919 Crosfields and Lever came together.

1929 saw the merger of Lever Bros Ltd with the Dutch Margarine Union to become Unilever.

The 'Persil Washes Whiter' theme was launched in the early days of the Second World War. As washing machines became more widely used, so washing powders had to change. The Persil of the 1950s was very different to the original one. In 1968 the biological powders were being launched, to be followed by the Persil Automatic powder.

Above *Persil in the 1950s*

Left *A Sunlight soap advert from 1906*

maclaren

Owen Finlay Maclaren MBE was already a retired aeronautical designer and former test pilot when he set about designing a new form of pushchair, the baby buggy.

He had been involved in the design of the Spitfire undercarriage before the Second World War and therefore knew a thing or two about lightweight, rigid, load-bearing structures capable of folding neatly.

When years later he was pushing his grandchild around in a clumsy, heavy conventional pushchair, he decided to redesign it. He used modern lightweight materials like tubular aluminium, developing a structure that could comfortably carry even a large child and then fold into a space only a little bigger than that occupied by a rolled-up umbrella. The first buggy weighed just six pounds.

In 1965 he was granted a patent and two years later the first buggy was sold commercially, having been manufactured in converted stables. Owen Maclaren and his team came up with several 'firsts' in baby transport – one of the most notable was 'balloon' tyres in 1976, to cushion a baby's ride. The rubber for the tyres is made to a secret formula known to only a few people – today the same tyres are also used on golf and supermarket trollies.

Sadly, Owen Maclaren died in 1978, but his vision transformed baby transport and baby buggies are sold all over the world.

Owen Maclaren (above) *used his aircraft design experience in developing his baby buggies*

Left *The Minor, the original aluminium umbrella-fold pushchair, updated for the 1990s*

Yeast, barm or leaven resulting from fermentation has been known for countless centuries. Justus Liebig knew that yeast contained about 50% of protein which possessed highly nutritious properties – the problem was how to convert it into a palatable food product. Eventually he found that by allowing the yeast to undergo a process of self-digestion, followed by concentration, he obtained a product almost indistinguishable in appearance, smell and flavour from extract of meat. Liebig died in 1873.

In 1902 the Marmite Food Extract Company was formed – a company which was to have the biggest impact on the recovery and handling of surplus yeast. It had its birth, and life, at Burton-on-Trent in Staffordshire. It took its name from *marmite* – French for stewpot – a feature which still appears on Marmite labels. With the discovery of vitamins it was found that brewers' yeast was, and still is, the richest natural source of the vitamin B complex.

When the editors were compiling the *Oxford Dictionary of Modern English* in the 1930s they decided that the word Marmite should be included. The company wrote that they defined Marmite as:

'An extract from fresh brewers' yeast, rich in vitamin B complex. Used for culinary purposes, eg. for making soups etc., and also medicinally. (Trade Name)'

Franklin C 'Frank' Mars began selling candy in 1902 when he was nineteen years old. Eight years later he started a wholesale candy business in Tacoma, Washington.

Around 1920, Mars moved to Minneapolis. There he started making butter creams in the family kitchen and these were delivered to shops in the city by his wife, Ethel. Two years later the Mar-O-Bar Company was founded to make quality confectionery bar products. Its first year, to many, would have been considered a disaster – whilst he employed fifteen people, he lost $6,000.

However, the following year the MILKY WAY Bar(known as the MARS Bar outside the USA) was introduced and quickly became a national success. The SNICKERS Bar (originally known as MARATHON in the United Kingdom) was launched as a summer product without a chocolate coating. Sales rose to $793,000!

The company was now growing rapidly and had become Mars Incorporated. Such was the pressure on the Minneapolis factory and its staff of 250 that a new site had to be found for a larger manufacturing plant. Frank Mars selected a Chicago suburb, believing that a residential area would offer more favourable transportation, lower raw material costs, and superior living conditions which would attract better workers – all promoting better quality! Production at the new plant got underway in 1929.

The following year the SNICKERS Bar was reintroduced, this time with a chocolate coating, and it became a great success.

In 1932 Frank's son, Forrest E Mars, left America for the United Kingdom, bringing with him the recipe for the MARS Bar. He rented a small factory in Slough where, with the help of about a dozen employees, they made MARS Bars by hand. They were sold locally for 2d each.

In the 1930s, when block chocolate was the most popular confectionery, the MARS Bar with its nougat and caramel filling was unique. It quickly became very popular, and after only six months the staff had to be doubled to help meet the demand.

The MILKY WAY Bar was introduced in 1935, followed shortly afterwards by MALTESERS chocolates. After the end of the Second World War they started to make sugar confectionery.

Mars products are now sold in over 150 countries worldwide. In the United Kingdom they are one of the country's largest confectionery companies.

Mars is still a privately-owned company.

Marvellous that anything so nice can be so full of real goodness too. But, as you see, Mars bars are packed with all those good things that nourish, energise and sustain you.

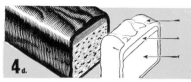

milk chocolate coating.

caramel layer of sugar, malt, glucose and milk.

delicious centre of malt, chocolate, glucose and sugar — all whipped in white of egg.

MAX FACTOR

In 1904, Max Factor, a Polish-born immigrant, arrived in New York from Moscow, where he had been the chief make-up artist at the Moscow Art Theatre.

The family settled in St Louis, Missouri, where a son, also called Max, was born later in the year. In St Louis, Max Factor Snr opened a perfume, make-up and hair goods concession at the St Louis World's Fair. Later in 1908, the family travelled west to Los Angeles and opened another theatrical shop for stage actors. On the 2nd January 1909, Max Factor & Co was formed.

At this time, the film industry was in its infancy and not the least of its problems was make-up. After much research, he perfected and produced the first make-up created specifically for film use.

In 1916, Max Factor decided to start manufacturing and selling to the ordinary woman. It was he who decided to adopt the word 'make-up' for his line of ordinary cosmetics. The company established a reputation as the 'House of Firsts'. Following Supreme Greasepaint came Colour Harmony – the matching of make-up to complexion and hair colour.

Left *Max Factor and 1930s movie star Jean Harlow*

This 1937 advert (below) also used film stars of the day

Max Factor,
Hollywood and London,

take this opportunity of expressing their loyalty to the Throne and offering their sincere felicitations for a long and prosperous reign.

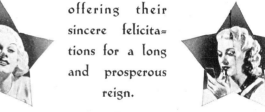

JEAN HARLOW
M.G.M. STAR

GINGER ROGERS
RADIO PICTURES STAR

★

1936—Accession Year—saw the foundation of Max Factor London Organisation

MERLE OBERON
UNITED ARTISTS STAR

Max Factor

MADELEINE CARROLL
PARAMOUNT STAR

HOLLYWOOD & LONDON (SALES) LIMITED
16 OLD BOND STREET, LONDON, W.1
REGENT 6720 (6 lines)

MCVITIE'S

Robert McVitie was born in 1809, growing up in Dumfries. He served an apprenticeship with a Scottish baker,

There are no Digestive Biscuits nicer than MCVITIE'S

—they are nourishing and sustaining too

Made from Dairy fresh Butter and

Home Grown Wheat

MADE BY MCVITIE & PRICE

before setting up in business at 150 Rose Street, Edinburgh, a tenement house owned by his father. From this start in 1830 the business became firmly established as a high-quality retail bakery and confectionery business, with several branches in the city.

One of his four children, also Robert, became an apprentice in the business and was later sent to France and Austria to study baking and confectionery – the business was later described as the 'Boulangerie Francaise et Viennoise'.

Young Robert set out to expand the business, building up sales outlets not only through Scotland but also in England. Because, in those days, bread would not keep very long, the company increasingly produced biscuits for their long-distance customers.

In 1887, Alexander Grant joined the firm. He was a baker who had learned his trade in Forres, Morayshire. He had marched in to see Robert McVitie, declaring he could make better scones than those on display in the window. Robert let him try, and the young man proved his point.

In 1888, Charles Price, one of the McVitie salesmen, was made a partner and the company became McVitie and Price. In 1892, Alexander Grant developed the first Digestive biscuit, and it has been made to the same recipe for almost 100 years. It was originally called Digestive because it contains baking soda which is known to help control flatulence – a product with this 'medicinal' ingredient was felt to aid the digestive system. In 1893 the firm was commissioned to provide a wedding cake for the marriage of the Duke of York and Princess Mary (later King George V and Queen Mary), thus beginning a tradition of supplying royal celebration cakes which lasts to this day.

By 1939 they were reported to be manufacturing 370 different varieties of biscuits and cakes. Since then they have been joined by other well known Scottish bakers – MacFarlane Lang & Co, MacDonalds, Crawfords, and Meredith and Drew, all working together under the McVitie's banner, today a division of United Biscuits.

In 1946, MacDonalds launched a chocolate-covered oblong cream biscuit which they named Penguin. It is regarded as a memorable and fun

name, and it has led to eye-catching and amusing packaging designs, also giving entertaining advertising opportunities, such as the well-known 'p-p-p-p-Pick up a Penguin'.

One of the company's most recent successes has been the introduction of the Hob-nob biscuit in the 1980s. It started a trend towards oat-based biscuits with a homebaked appearance and taste. Its name comes from 'Hob' as in ovens, and 'nob' as in a nob of butter.

Above *Penguin was launched in 1946 – here it is in 1952*

Left *This 1934 McVities advert was simple and direct*

MONOPOLY

Registered Trade Mark

Although John Waddington was an apprentice printer, he was in some ways more suited to the ways of the theatre. At the turn of the century he started a printing business at Camp Road, Leeds, printing theatre posters and other material. John Waddington Ltd was formed in 1905 – among the shareholders was Fred Karno! John Waddington pressed his fellow directors for money to buy lithographic machinery, and Victor Watson was invited to become lithographic foreman. Money difficulties became more severe and finally, in 1913, John Waddington resigned. Victor Watson was appointed general manager.

In 1916, Victor Watson was appointed a director, and the company was made public in 1921, the same year that the playing card manufacture was put on a firm basis. 1934 was to see the beginning of a new game which would be an outstanding success – Monopoly.

Monopoly had been developed around 1930 by Charles B Darrow of Germantown, Pennsylvania, USA. In the depression years of the 1930s, many Americans could only pretend to deal in big money and expensive property because of the financial recession.

Prior to this, in 1929 after the Wall Street crash, Charles Darrow, an unemployed equipment salesman, displayed great initiative and ambition by mending old irons, walking dogs

and mowing lawns. At night time he invented new ideas in toys and games.

Then came 'The Game', as his family called it in the early days, what we now know as Monopoly. In its earliest days it consisted of a board made out of oil-cloth, coloured with free paint samples from a local store, houses and

The pioneer of Monopoly, Charles B Darrow

hotels cut out of beading picked up from a lumber yard, with the title cards made from old cardboard. The street names were real streets in Atlantic City, where in earlier years and better times Darrow used to spend the summer with his family. It is said that the tokens were charms from his wife's bracelet.

A similar game had received a patent in Virginia in 1924, but in Darrow's

game, complete sets of properties must be acquired before houses or hotels can be 'built'. Probably it is this feature which has helped to make it the best of all property-trading board games.

Darrow's game pleased his family and friends so much that he was soon asked to make one or two sets a day. Demand grew and so he contracted out the board production to a jobbing printer, increasing his output to six sets a day. When department stores began ordering it wholesale (the John Wananmaker department store in Philadelphia was the first in 1934), he had to decide how to expand production. He approached Parker Brothers of Salem, Massachusetts, an established games company, but they rejected it, saying it contained fifty-two fundamental errors. Undaunted, he went home and continued to make Monopoly; working 14 hours a day, he produced 20,000 sets that year.

Of course Parker Brothers soon heard about this and decided to offer Darrow an attractive royalty – which he gladly accepted. He later retired at the age of forty-six and died a multi-millionaire aged seventy-eight.

In the early part of 1935, Parkers sent a sample to Waddingtons. One Friday night, the head of the company, Victor Watson Snr, handed his son Norman (who was managing the playing card division) the set with the remarks: 'Look this over and tell me what you think of it.'

He played an imaginary game against himself, continuing through Friday night, Saturday night and Sunday night. He was enthralled and captivated. So enthusiastic was he that on the Monday morning he persuaded his father to telephone Parker Brothers – it was the first transatlantic telephone call Waddingtons had ever made – resulting in them granting John Waddington Ltd a licence to manufacture Monopoly. The American placenames were changed – Victor Watson's secretary, Marjory Phillips, was asked to take a walk round London to get the right names – and the dollars became pounds. Otherwise the rules were the same.

During the war, the War Office commissioned Waddingtons to make up intricate games and playing cards which would, if properly used, give help to prisoners of war. The company soon realised the significance of the phrase 'if properly used'. In one side of the board was inserted a map, printed on silk, showing the escape routes from the particular prison to which the game was sent. In the other side, small holes were cut in which a compass and several fine-quality files were placed; and the Monopoly money was actual German, Austrian or Italian money!

There are now world records for the longest games, the smallest board and the largest game – using real streets; it has even been played underwater! A world championship was held for Monopoly's fortieth anniversary in 1975, and every few years since. In 1972, a plan to change some of Atlantic City's street names – the basis of the Monopoly streets – was defeated by the public outcry from players across America and from Parker Brothers.

Today Monopoly is licensed in 32 countries by Parker Brothers, being translated into no less than 17 languages, with the use of local place names and currencies.

Above   *The first UK Monopoly set in 1935 cost 7s 6d and had cardboard figures*

Left   *The 1984 British Monopoly championship was played with a gold-plated set – and with real money!*

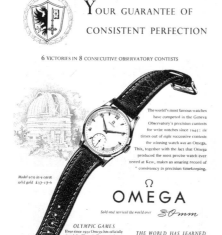

OMEGA

This 1950s model was in nine carat gold, costing over £37

Louis Brandt was twenty-three years old when he created an assembly workshop at La Chaux-de-Fonds, Switzerland. He made key-wound precision pocket watches in silver cases, which he then sold throughout Europe from Italy to Scandinavia, but his most important market was England.

In 1877, Louis Brandt entered into a partnership with his eldest son Louis Paul, thus founding the company Louis Brandt and Fils. Three years later, Louis Paul and his brother Cesar established the company in Bienne and started producing all their own watch components. Five years later they introduced the lever escapement, with a precision of .30 seconds a day. By 1889 they were already the largest Swiss watchmakers, with 600 employees producing 100,000 watches a year.

It was in 1894 that the name of Omega was introduced – it was the idea of Henri Rieckel, banker to the Brandt brothers. Omega (literally 'great o') is the twenty-fourth and last letter of the Greek alphabet. In the revelation to John in the Bible, we find:

'I am the Alpha and the Omega, the first and the last, the beginning and the end.'

Omega is synonymous with accomplishment, completion, achievement, perfection. Omega was the name given to their nineteen line calibre, remarkable for the perfection of its construction and the modesty of its price. In 1896 the Omega watch received a gold medal at the Swiss National Exhibition in Geneva.

1909 saw the first sports timing, the Gordon Bennett Cup for balloons in Zurich. In 1917 the British Royal Flying Corps chose the Omega watches for their combat units,

Astronaut Thomas P Stafford wearing an Omega

followed in 1918 by the American Army. In 1932 Omega was used for the first time at an Olympic Games. Throughout all the succeeding years their watches have been used in prestigious events and received the highest results in performance competitions. At the 1952 Helsinki Olympic Games they introduced quartz technology, thus launching electronic timekeeping. They were awarded the Olympic Cross of Merit for yet another development, the Omegascope – each contestant's time filmed

Louis Brandt, the father of the company

by the television camera and printed on a screen.

Neil Armstrong wore a Speedmaster chronograph when he became the first man to walk on the moon on the 21st July 1969. NASA presented Omega with the Snoopy Award, their highest distinction.

The introduction of the first LED digital display, the 'time computer', came in 1973. But excellence in performance has not been their only aim or achievement. Over the years they have also received the most coveted awards for styling, especially in fine jewellery watches.

OVALTINE

Dr George Wander, a Swiss chemist, set up a laboratory in Berne in 1865. This was the start of a pharmaceutical and dietary industry which has spread throughout the world.

This 1975 advert reconstructed the original 1930s Ovaltineys Club

His early work was to investigate the nutritional values of barley malt. It was at his laboratory that he made a tasty malt extract which became increasingly popular. Successive products based on the use of this malt extract culminated in 1904 with the launching of a product now known all over the world under the name of Ovomaltine or Ovaltine. Doctors recognised its high nutritional value, and it was quickly a success both in Switzerland and in the export markets which rapidly followed.

The company in the United Kingdom was founded in 1909, but initially Ovaltine was shipped in bulk from Switzerland. In 1913, a small factory at King's Langley was opened, with a staff of four girls in the packing room and a total of under twenty employees.

In the 1920s the company grew rapidly, erecting the main buildings as they appear today. In 1929 the Ovaltine Farm was established, covering an area of over 400 acres, and supplying milk and eggs for the manufacture of Ovaltine.

Imaginative advertising, incorporating the Ovaltine Dairy Maid and the Ovaltiney Club, led to greater sales and public awareness of the product.

In 1935 the Ovaltiney Club, sponsored by the company, was launched on Radio Luxembourg. It was broadcast on Sunday evenings between 5.30 pm and 6pm. The club's song *We are the Ovaltineys* became perhaps the most evocative jingle of all time, and by 1939 there were 5,000,000 active club members. After more than two hundred shows, the programme was suspended when the Second World War closed Radio Luxembourg. In 1946 it reappeared and ran for several more years. In 1975, after popular demand, the company brought back the original *We are the Ovaltineys* song by incorporating it into a television commercial.

Nowadays, 100 million cups of Ovaltine are drunk each year.

A CUP of 'Ovaltine' at bedtime helps to relax nervous tensions and promote the conditions favourable to natural, refreshing sleep. Made from Nature's best foods, its valuable nutritive properties, including additional vitamins, assist in providing the nourishment to restore the tired body and rebuild strength and vitality.

For these reasons delicious 'Ovaltine' has long been the regular bedtime beverage in countless homes throughout the world. There is nothing like it.

No other beverage can give you better sleep

1/6, 2/6 and 4/6 per tin

Ovaltine was the 'National Beverage for Health' in 1937 ... and 'The World's Best Nightcap' in 1954

◈ PARKER

In 1636, William Parker left Dover with his wife Mary and set sail for the New World. They settled in Connecticut, New England.

William's descendants seem to have inherited his spirit of adventure. George Parker was born in 1863 at Shullsberg in Wisconsin, but while he was still small his parents packed all their belongings in a covered wagon and drove to a farm near Fayette, in Iowa. Here he had to work long hours in the fields, only attending school in the winter when he could be spared from the farm.

George Parker

However, he successfully matriculated from Upper Iowa University and began thinking about a career. Farming was ruled out, but he wondered about a career on the railway or in medicine, that was until he saw an advertisement for the Valentine School of Telegraphy. This advertisement convinced him – he saved up the $55 for the fees and enrolled. Within a year he was on the staff!

The salary was far from adequate, so George took on a part-time job as the local representative of the John Holland Fountain Pen Company. The pens were poor, and being in regular contact with students, he had to face the criticism. He recognised that the problem was the feed-shaft. With a scroll saw, a file and some other simple equipment he made a shaft that would let the air up more steadily. To start with, he put the improved shafts in the pens he was selling, but when he realised how much he had improved the product he decided he might as well be selling his own pens. With just the few dollars he could spare he bought a supply of hard rubber tube and ordered some other parts from manufacturing jobbers; he started up the manufacture in the bedroom of the hotel where he was living. This was the beginning of Parker Pens, in 1886.

The next step was to take out a patent. He then got a firm to make some fountain pens for him, in one gross lots, each one stamped 'Geo. S. Parker'. He got some commercial travellers he knew to take out his pens as a sideline to their main business.

In 1889 he patented the first 'jointless' pen – no thread to wear, no nozzle to get stuck, and no joint to leak. It was the first Parker pen to be advertised in the United Kingdom, in time for that year's Christmas sales.

He marketed ink under his own name before the First World War, but it was the introduction of Quink Ink in 1931

The first UK advert for the Parker 'Jointless Lucky Curve' pen

that is best remembered. That year a Christmas pack was distributed to dealers – it contained a Duofold pen and pencil set and a free sample bottle of Quink Ink, the ink being scented! It sold 558,000 sets.

In 1930, George Parker said:

'It is my earnest wish to share the blessings God has given me with my helpers, in order that they enjoy some of the refinements of life which they might not otherwise have.'

He died in 1937.

The famous arrow clip on all the pens was designed by Joseph Platt, a talented New York artist whom George Parker's son, Kenneth, specially commissioned. It first appeared in 1932 and variations on the design have been used ever since. As far as is known, the choice of the arrow motif seems to have been dictated by the functional requirements of an effective clip. In the early 1960s, the motif was incorporated into the company's logo.

The Parker 51 came out of development in 1939 – 51 years after the first Parker was launched. It became the flagship of the post-war years and was one of the best pens Parker ever designed.

The Parker 51 was the ideal Christmas gift in 1950

Pears

Andrew Pears, the son of a Cornish farmer, completed his apprenticeship as a hairdresser in 1789 and, seeing little future in his native village of Mevagissey, made his way to London where he established himself as a hairdresser in Gerrard Street, Soho. Andrew also manufactured rouges, creams, powders and other beauty aids in his shop.

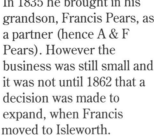

Andrew Pears

He found that his products were often needed to repair the harm caused by the harsh soaps used at the time, and so he began experimenting to make a soap which would be more gentle on delicate complexions. Finally he produced a soap which was infinitely superior to any on the market by refining the base soap and removing its harshness and impurities. Not only was this soap of high quality, but it also had the novelty of being delicately perfumed (with the flowers of an English garden) and also being transparent.

Andrew Pears continued caring for his clients' hair and compounding beauty preparations, but now his main interest was in manufacturing and selling the soap he had invented. His business began to prosper as his reputation grew and the demand for his soap increased. Rivals soon began to make cheap imitations of Pears Soap and its wrappings, but they could not discover the secret formula. Andrew was more concerned about his reputation for his quality soap than for his loss of trade and so he announced that he would sign each packet with 'my own quill', thus exposing 'those fraudulent practices'.

In 1835 he brought in his grandson, Francis Pears, as a partner (hence A & F Pears). However the business was still small and it was not until 1862 that a decision was made to expand, when Francis moved to Isleworth.

Francis Pears' eldest daughter, Mary, married Thomas J Barratt. It was he who brought marketing skills and became an international figure in the relatively new profession of advertising, and made Pears Soap well known throughout the world.

The basis of Barratt's sales appeal was that Pears Soap was safe and healthy and that it made its users beautiful. He also turned to 'glamour' advertising. He made Mrs Lily Langtry, the actress friend of Edward VII, his first star by obtaining testimonials from her about Pears Soap:

'Since using Pears Soap, I have discarded all others.'

When this started to lose its appeal he used a cartoon by Harry Furniss showing a disreputable unwashed tramp laboriously writing his testimonial to Pears:

'Two years ago I used your soap, since when I have used no other.'

It was originally in *Punch*, making fun of Mrs Langtry's testimonial but was used to the company's benefit.

Around 1880, Barratt initiated one of his most fantastic schemes. At the time there were many French ten centime pieces in circulation in England and these were accepted as the equivalent of English pennies. He imported about a quarter of a million of these pieces and, as there was no law forbidding it, he defaced them by having the name Pears stamped on each one. He then put them into circulation. This led to an act of Parliament which declared all foreign coins to be illegal tender, and they were withdrawn.

The most famous example of Barratt's new approach to advertising was a painting known as *Bubbles*. Sir John

Everett Millais, President of the Royal Academy, painted a portrait of his grandson watching a soap bubble he had just blown through a clay pipe. It was first exhibited at the Royal Academy, then sold to the *Illustrated London News* for reproduction in their magazine. Pears bought it from the *Illustrated London News* for £2,200 to use as an advertisement.

The Miss Pears competition was first introduced in 1958. The winner becomes a 'princess for the day', and has her portrait painted by a popular artist of the time. The competition now attracts 20,000 entries every year.

In 1914 the firm joined Lever Brothers and today is part of Elida Gibbs, the toiletries division of Unilever.

"Two years ago I used your soap, since when I have used no other."
—*Punch*, April 26th, 1884.

"For years I have used your soap, and no other."

Lily Langtry's tribute to Pears soap (right), *and* Punch's *spoof*

Bubbles *was by Sir John Millais of his grandson, and became Pears' most famous advert*

Harbutt's Plasticine®

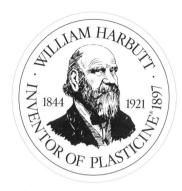

William Harbutt was born in 1844 at Newcastle-upon-Tyne. Later he was sent to study at South Kensington Art School where he became an artist of considerable skill. At the age of thirty he moved to Bath to take over the headmastership of the old Bath School of Art. His progressive ideas did not fit in with those of the committee and in 1877 he resigned, establishing his own art school in Bath and subsequently becoming art master at most of the local schools in a private capacity.

It was one of his problems as an art teacher which then led him to found a new industry. The clay used for modelling was a heavy and difficult material for budding art students to use, and so William set about creating a new material.

Small-scale production started with the help of an old soldier, the material being made in tubs in the basement of his home, using hands and arms to do the mixing. When a certain stage was reached, a heavy garden roller was pushed backwards and forwards over the mixture for about five minutes until the right consistency was obtained. The water squeezed out was mopped up by rags, and the mixture then squeezed through a fine dye plate and laid out to dry and mature for several weeks. It is said there are still traces of Plasticine to be found in cracks and crevices of this house, even today.

Like many inventors with families, William allowed his children to play with the new grey material which modelled so easily, and they were fascinated. This gave William food for thought. Up until then he had thought of his invention as a teaching aid, but now began to consider its merits for children's creative enjoyment.

Now a name was clearly required; the whole family put their heads together and the name Plasticine emerged.

At first, Plasticine was only available in grey, but William continued with his developments and produced a three colour pack of red, blue and yellow called 'The Complete Modeller'. Trade enquiries began coming in, and William was launched into business.

In May 1900, production began at an old flour mill at Bathampton, near Bath, which William had bought. His daughter Olive began to travel round the country with him, demonstrating his product; and soon they were travelling to Australia and the USA.

In 1912 a limited company was formed. William Harbutt died in 1921, and is buried in Bathampton churchyard. William's family carried on the business.

Plasticine had many uses. In the First World War, the chief modeller, Albert Blanchard, was asked to make a scale model of the country around Vimy Ridge by the military authorities. The racer Sir Malcolm Campbell used a specially-built Plasticine racing car in a wind tunnel to discover its faults.

Today Plasticine is a household word in many countries, and is a worldwide registered trademark.

A bas-relief frieze of horses by William Harbutt's daughter Olive, made in 1910

PRETTY POLLY

The company of Hibbert and Buckland was started in 1920. One of their earliest customers was a wholesaler in Leek, Staffordshire, whose brand name at that time was Pretty Polly. Around 1926 the wholesaler withdrew from the business, so Hibbert and Buckland obtained the brand name and traded under the Pretty Polly name from that time.

The reason for the original wholesaler using the name was that the company was owned by a successful bookmaker. In 1904 the famous filly, Pretty Polly, won three out of five English Classic races and it had brought him considerable fortune. When he handed the company over to his daughter he suggested the name 'Pretty Polly' be used. It is rumoured that, at the time, he said to his daughter:

'If this name is as successful for you, as it always was for me, you will come to no harm.'

A print of a painting of the horse is displayed at the company headquarters.

The advent of nylon in 1946 saw the company steadily expand. At that time production stood at 2,500 dozen pairs of stockings/tights per week, and by 1976 that figure had risen to 250,000 dozen pairs per week, putting them into the top four worldwide producers. Today the company exports to many countries spread throughout the world.

Pretty Polly won the Oaks, the 1,000 Guineas and the St Leger in 1904

It's like getting three dishes in one!

THE COMPLETE CASSEROLE
Modern, streamlined, practical, ideal for stews and ragouts, it will save you endless trouble. No hard-to-clean crevices, no dishing-up. The food comes straight from oven to table — piping hot.

THE LID. Turn it over and it becomes the very dish for a fruit tart, baked eggs, dozens of things. There are no awkward handles or knobs to break or catch on the oven shelves — just graceful, easy-to-grip wings.

THE BOTTOM PART. Used without the lid it is invaluable for such things as shepherd's pie, macaroni cheese, and bread-and-butter puddings. You can *see* the food cooking in "Pyrex" Brand dishes.

"Pyrex" Brand Streamline Oval Casserole (S283)

Only 5/6 — and it lasts for years!

BESIDES doing the work of three useful dishes at the cost of one, every "Pyrex" Brand Streamline Casserole saves you money in other ways. It economises on gas (because food heats evenly and more quickly in glass), and it lasts indefinitely without getting shabby, chipped or cracked.

And that's true of all the other lovely "Pyrex" Brand dishes! Ask to see them at any good glass or hardware shop or department store — you'll like their handsome and practical designs in many shapes and sizes.

And another thing — it pays to insist on getting genuine "Pyrex" Brand, because each piece of "Pyrex" Brand glassware carries a 12 months' *Free Replacement Guarantee* against breakage by oven heat. James A. Jobling and Co. Ltd., Wear Glass Works, Sunderland.

REGISTERED TRADE MARK **"PYREX"** BRAND
streamline **casserole**

THE FIRST — THE BEST — TESTED AND PROVED IN A MILLION OVENS

A 1937 advert showing the many uses of the new Pyrex oven dishes

Otto Schott, a German, is generally credited as being the father of modern glass technology. He recognised the commercial potential of borosilicate glass, a glass made with silica and boron oxide as its main components. The resultant glass can withstand both rapid changes of temperature and also attacks from chemicals. It is therefore ideal for use in cooking utensils and also for glassware in laboratories.

Corning Glassworks, a US company, used this pioneering work of Dr Schott at the beginning of this century. They were able to produce a successful borosilicate glass which was known as Nonex. This was introduced in 1912. The following year the wife of one of Corning's researchers baked a cake in a cut-down Nonex battery jar, making this the first domestic use of borosilicate glass.

In 1915 the company developed the first commercial application of borosilicate glass for domestic use and gave it the name Pyrex.

In 1858, James Angus and Henry Greener had acquired the Wear Flint Glass Works in Sunderland. By 1882 the business was unprofitable, and in 1886 the firm was taken over by its principal creditor, James Augustus Jobling, a Newcastle-upon-Tyne businessman and one of the largest mineral merchants and suppliers of glassmaking chemicals in the North of England. It was his nephew, Ernest Jobling Purser, who in 1921 saw through the purchase of the sole rights to manufacture Pyrex products in the British Empire, with the exception of Canada.

Having acquired the rights, they immediately started to manufacture laboratory wares and casserole dishes, selling them under the name Pyrex. During the 1920s and 1930s, Jobling's range of Pyrex borosilicate domestic wares expanded to cover pie and roasting dishes, dinner and fruit sets – even tea pots!

Between 1946 and 1958 the production of Pyrex increased by 94%. When Joblings took over the company, the works covered one acre; by the 1950s the area had increased to over 40 acres.

In 1952, Pyrex Colourware was introduced, being followed two years later by Opalware.

In 1954, Corning acquired a 40% share in Joblings, taking up the remainder of the shares in 1973. Today Corning Ltd is the leading manufacturer of speciality glass. Since 1908 they have been at the forefront of development in glass technology. As well as their work with resistant domestic glassware, they have also developed photochromatic lenses for the use in prescriptive spectacles and sunglasses, and high performance windows for US spacecraft. They employ about 300,000 people in factories spread through many parts of the world, including the USA, Canada, France, Australia, Japan and Great Britain.

It was the advice of a doctor which led Frank Bowden to a bicycle workshop on Russell Street in Nottingham. While working as a law clerk in Hong Kong, the debilitating climate nearly killed him. He returned to England in 1886 with a moderate fortune and ruined health. His doctor advised him to try

One of the very first Raleigh bicycles in 1887

cycling – his health immediately improved. The cycle firm of Woodhead, Angois and Ellis was originally founded in nearby Raleigh Street, but had moved to larger premises in Russell Street by the time Frank Bowden took an interest in 1887 on seeing the potential of the bicycle.

The Raleigh Cycle Company was founded in December 1888, and by December 1891 the company had a capital of £100,000; within five years this had doubled, such was the growth.

In 1896 a new factory was built on a seven and a half acre site in Faraday Road, Nottingham. It was the largest in the country and gave employment to 850 people. Originally the workshop in Raleigh Street had employed twelve men who produced three cycles a week; by the turn of the century the company was producing 12,000 cycles a year.

Frank Bowden's flair for assessing new devices led him to an interest in Sturmey-Archer and Pellant variable gears, and in 1903 the manufacture and marketing of the hub gears was taken over by Raleigh through the formation of its first subsidiary, Sturmey-Archer Gears Limited.

In the 1920s the Raleigh name also became famous for motorcycles, and in the early 1930s for the then quite revolutionary three wheel light car and delivery vans. These were discontinued by 1936 to meet the tremendous demand for bicycles.

By 1957 the factory covered no less than sixty-four acres, but then a period of severe contraction was to follow when production fell

Raleigh branched out into motorcycles in the 1920s

This portrait of Sir Frank Bowden was presented to him by his employees to commemorate his seventieth birthday in 1918 – and the thirtieth anniversary of Raleigh

from 4 million to 2 million. Later a new trend in cycle design came with the introduction of the small-wheeled bicycle, the RSW 16. June 1970 saw the introduction of the Chopper and 1976 the Grifter, which resembled a scrambler motorbike.

The record breaker

ROBERTSON'S

James Robertson started work as a thread mill worker in Paisley, but seeing little hope for the future he joined a local grocer as an apprentice for twelve shillings a week.

However his ambition led him to open his own grocery store, where in 1864 he was persuaded by a salesman to purchase a barrel of bitter oranges. Sales of the oranges proved to be very slow, and it would have been ruinous for the tiny business if they could not have been disposed of quickly. His wife, Marion, offered a solution by suggesting that she should make the oranges into marmalade, an idea which proved so popular that the preserving pans in her kitchen were inadequate to cope with the demand.

Beginning in a rented section of a local cloth finishing works, where the surplus steam was utilised to heat the preserving pans, the business progressed over a two year period to the stage where it was necessary to move to a separate factory.

Marion Robertson is credited with having coined the name 'Golden Shred' for her unique clear marmalade. A lemon marmalade was later introduced with the name of 'Silver Shred', followed by a range of other marmalades and jams.

During the nineteenth century the business grew steadily, and sales gradually extended from Scotland to the whole of Great Britain.

Robertson products are very clearly associated with their famous 'Golly' trademark, which originated just before the First World War, when a Robertson director visiting America came upon the Golly and thought it would make an appealing mascot and

A 1952 advert for Robertson's Golden Shred

trademark for Robertson's products. Soon afterwards the Golly design was incorporated into every product label bearing the Robertson name.

In 1930 the first enamel Golly brooches and badges were made, commencing with the Golly Golfer; since then over 15 million have been given away.

The Passing of an Old-time custom

The practice of making Mincemeat at home is rapidly becoming a thing of the past. The long and tedious task of preparing the ingredients is avoided in the modern custom of using

'Golden Shred' Mincemeat

NOTE: Golden Shred Mincemeat should not be confused with butcher's minced beef. It is made from selected fruits . . . oriental spices . . . pure white sugar . . . nothing else.

Excellent for puddings, tarts, Eccles cakes and similar dainty dishes. Guaranteed by Robertson's to contain only the best ingredients.

This December 1928 advert notes that Golden Shred Mincemeat 'should not be confused with butcher's minced beef'

Rowntree Mackintosh

Mary Tuke was a Quaker living in York. She opened a grocer's shop in the city, which by 1785 had begun to trade under the name of Wm Tuke & Sons, also selling cocoa.

In 1815 the firm described themselves as tea dealers, adding that they sold roasted coffee and manufactured chocolate. In 1862, Henry Isaac Rowntree acquired the cocoa and chocolate side of the business. This expanded so quickly that he decided to buy a foundry in York and convert it into a cocoa and chocolate manufacturing plant. In 1869, Henry's brother, Joseph, became his partner and the company became H I Rowntree & Co.

Henry Rowntree

John Mackintosh in 1931

Ten years later they started to manufacture pastilles and gums, which at that time had been a monopoly of the French. Indeed it was a Frenchman, Monsieur Gaget, who took charge of the new department and Rowntree's Fruit Pastilles were introduced in 1881. In 1882 they bought and converted a flour mill in York, the company then making rock cocoa, a mixture of fine cocoa mixed with sugar, which was sold in blocks; loose cocoa powder, mixed with arrowroot or sago; and also chocolate drops, chocolate beans, and penny and halfpenny balls.

In 1890 the company bought the land upon which the York factory now stands. Today the works and their surrounding areas occupy nearly 141 acres.

Rowntree's Fruit Gums were introduced in 1893. By 1897 the firm was employing 1,200 workers, but by 1909 this had risen quickly to a staggering 4,000.

In 1901 Rowntree's Table Jellies were introduced, and in the 1930s several new lines were created, including the well-known Black Magic in 1933. 7,000 typical consumers were interviewed before it was developed, the aim being to find out their conception of a perfect chocolate assortment. The final twelve centres were selected from hundreds tested. The pack remained the same for the next thirty-eight years. Kit Kat (then Chocolate Crisp) and Aero were introduced in 1935, Dairy Box in 1936, with Smarties in 1937. Polo came along in 1948 and After Eight in 1962.

Creamola Food Products and Sun Pat Products Ltd joined Rowntree in the 1960s, and in

John Mackintosh's original shop in King Cross Lane, Halifax, 1890

1969 a major merger took place when Rowntree & Co Ltd joined with John Mackintosh & Sons Ltd to form Rowntree Mackintosh Ltd.

In 1890, John Mackintosh had opened a confectionery shop in King Cross Lane, Halifax, a few days after his marriage to Violet Taylor. His intention was to 'offer only articles extra specially good in an establishment that was spotlessly clean'. He soon decided that a new attraction was needed to increase his takings. His idea was to combine brittle English butter-

Quality Street is still manufactured in Halifax, and today it is the world's biggest assortment – being exported to over 100 countries.

Mackintosh merged with Rowntree in 1969, and in 1988 Rowntree Mackintosh joined Nestlé SA, the world's largest food company.

A 1936 advert

scotch with soft American caramel to produce a high quality toffee. The resultant product was named 'Mackintosh's Celebrated Toffee'. He invited the public of Halifax to taste a free sample, and long before closing time they were sold out. A second advertisement appeared within a matter of days:

'On Saturday last you were eating Mackintosh's toffee at our expense; next Saturday pay us another visit and eat it at your own expense.'

The result of this advertisement was overwhelming. Before long the toffee sales far outstripped the cakes, pies and other articles sold. People from all over Halifax came to the 'Toffee Shop', and soon retailers from other parts of the North of England began to sell Mackintosh's Toffee. In 1899 they moved to Queens Road, but this factory was destroyed by fire in 1909. As a result of this they moved to Albion Mills, near the railway station,

and this became their permanent headquarters.

It was in 1936 that the greatest introduction was to come – Quality Street. The brand name originated from the play *Quality Street* written by J M Barrie, the author of *Peter Pan*. The product's identity was based on the play's main characters, a soldier and his young lady. Shopkeepers were urged to stock the new product with the slogan: 'Put *your* shop in Quality Street, by putting Quality Street in your shop'. It is still distinguished from other brands by its wide variety of shapes and the bright design of its wrappings.

Scholl

William Mathias Scholl was born in 1882 on a small dairy farm near La Porte, Indiana, the third son in a line of thirteen children. As a boy he saw many farmers and housewives forced into a life of semi-idleness because of foot problems, which also caused people much discomfort.

He became apprenticed to the local shoemaker, then left the farmlands of

The Foot Specialist

VOL. IV   EDITED BY DR. WM. M. SCHOLL   NO. 9
September 1917

The Most Prized Comforter in the Comfort Kit~

Indiana to work in a shoe shop in Chicago. He soon realised that no two feet are alike and therefore each foot presents an individual fitting problem. He also learned that minor foot troubles could be greatly aggravated by the wrong shoes. In many instances the structure of the foot could not assume its natural function in standing or walking – nature needed help if relief was to be provided.

To further his knowledge, William enrolled at one of the best-known medical schools in America. He soon engaged in endless research and experimentation, making exhaustive studies of the anatomy and the relationship of the foot structure to the rest of the body. He examined the effect on the entire body of faulty foot structure. Now, armed with sound medical training and supported with practical experience, the young doctor designed his first arch support, in 1904.

He rented a cubbyhole in the rear of a shop in West Madison Street. He placed his bed in one corner out of view, and for months this single room

During the First World War, according to one report, Scholl products 'enabled soldiers to endure hard marches, stand for long periods and do excessive foot work with a minimum of pain and discomfort'

Dr Scholl's products have brought relief to millions of feet

served as a study, workshop, consulting room, fitting booth, office and living quarters. He did a brisk business and soon was able to hire craftsmen to fashion his leather and metal supports.

William Scholl toured stores selling his new product. With a foot skeleton, he would explain about foot anatomy, saying that his new 'Foot-Eazer' would 'restore the foot structure and re-educate the muscles'. In 1907 he developed corn plasters, which he called Absorbo Pads. About this time, the company's first national advertisement appeared – and the response convinced Scholl of the power of good advertising.

From such a small beginning the company grew rapidly, and by 1910 a branch was opened in Toronto. In that same year William's brother, Frank J Scholl, who had studied his brother's teaching and methods, came to the United Kingdom and set up a business in London. Soon Scholl expertise expanded into Europe – first to Belgium, then Holland, Germany, Sweden and beyond.

Today, Scholl products now include elastic hosiery, health footwear and many other lines – in addition to the extensive footcare range – which are sold in over a hundred countries.

This tiny workshop was where Scholl perfected his Foot-Eazer arch support

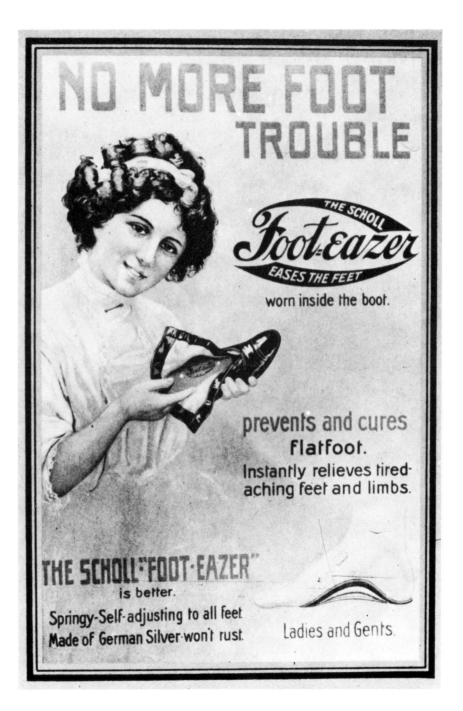

The Foot-Eazer figured in one of Scholl's earliest display cards

Scotch™

3M was born in July 1902. It was the idea of five businessmen who lived and worked in the area surrounding a small town called Two Harbours, in Minnesota. They were Henry Bryan and William McGonagle, both holding responsible positions in railroad companies; Dr Danley Budd, the Two Harbours general physician; Hermon Cable, owner of the local meat market; and John Dwan, a lawyer. They called themselves the Minnesota Mining & Manufacturing Co – the 3 Ms.

The company was formed to mine a mineral called corundum, but it transpired that the corundum was of only low quality. However, it was felt it could be used to make sandpaper. During the First World War they supplied abrasives to many industries involved in the war

'SCOTCH BOY'
Regd Trade Mark
THE ORIGINAL
CELLULOSE TAPE
Made by the Minnesota Mining & Manufacturing Co. Ltd, Adderley Park, Birmingham 8

Scotch tape was called Scotch Boy in 1953

effort. 1926 saw the introduction of a waterproof sandpaper.

In the late 1920s, Dick Drew, a laboratory researcher, started to look at a new kind of sticky tape. It came from a demand from within the automobile industry for a tape to use in the paint-spraying process to mask edges and separate colours on two-tone cars. There resulted six years of research before a satisfactory product was found, but in 1935 a 3M Masking Tape was introduced.

Following from this, Drew was asked to invent a tape that would stick paper wrappings around the insulation in refrigerators. The problem was how to make a tape that would stay stuck on when it got both cold and damp. Dupont had just invented Cellophane transparent film and Drew got hold of some samples. He tried coating the Cellophane film with adhesive, and after many trials he found a product that did work – this was the beginning of Scotch Clear Tape. The new product was introduced in 1931. America took to the tape like wild fire! By 1939 a separate factory had to be built to cope with demand, followed very soon after by second and third factories. In 1941, sales totalled $14 million.

But why the name 'Scotch'? The story goes that an angry auto body painter in the mid 1920s had trouble in making an early roll of two inch wide masking tape stick and noticed that it

Two of 3M's founders: Henry Bryan (left) was its first president, and John Dwan was the secretary

only had adhesive along its edges. He told the salesman:

'Take this tape back to your stingy Scotch bosses and tell them to put more adhesive on it.'

Whether the first batch of tape stuck or not, the name certainly did!

Other products which were to become part of our daily life were to follow. Together with Ampex and ABC Radio, 3M developed a plastic-backed magnetic tape. Later in the mid 1950s, 3M, Ampex and Bing Crosby Enterprises worked together to produce the world's first successful video recorder. 3M, of course, produced the tape, the start of yet another very important product – Scotch Magnetic VR tape.

Today 3M has operations in over fifty-two different countries, with a range of 60,000 different products. Sales worldwide are now $13 billion.

Jacob Schweppe was born in Witzenhausen, Germany, in 1740. When Jacob was eleven or twelve years old his parents, considering him to be too delicate for a life in agriculture, allowed a travelling tinker to take charge of him. The tinker soon recognised his talents – he mended pots so well – and so took him back to his parents and recommended that they placed him under a silversmith. This

Portrait based on a description of Jacob Schweppe during his stay in London, 1792–99

was done, and once again his skills were found to be outstanding. It was recommended that he be placed with a *bijouterie*, a more difficult branch of the profession.

In about 1765 he moved to Geneva, and in 1767 he married Eleonore Roget. Whilst continuing as a jeweller, he also followed his interest in scientific matters, particularly the aeration of water and production of artificial mineral waters. The waters he created were of such good quality that, rather

than letting them go to waste, he gave them to local doctors so that their poorer patients might have them without charge. The demand for his waters grew, and in the early 1780s he moved into commercial production. It would therefore seem reasonable to suggest that Jacob Schweppe was the founder of the soft drinks industry as we know it today.

In 1790, Jacob Schweppe entered into a partnership with three others and formed the company of Schweppe, Paul and Gosse. Attached to the prospectus for the new partnership was a statement saying that Jacob Schweppe had the idea of imitating natural mineral waters for about ten years and had manufactured seltzer and spa water for seven or eight years.

Jacob Schweppe arrived in England in 1792 and the first factory was set up at 141 Drury Lane, London. The venture was certainly not an immediate success, and it was one of the factors which led to the dissolving of the partnership in 1793. Jacob Schweppe retained the business in England, but lost all that he had worked so hard to develop in Geneva. The plant was modest, and firstly he moved it to King's Street, Holborn, before moving yet again in 1795 to Margaret Street, Cavendish Square, Westminster.

It was during the 1790s that the term 'Soda Water' came into use, and Schweppe's product was particularly recommended for the treatment of 'Stone of the bladder'. Soda water was named in a Schweppes advertisement of around 1798, and the use of this description ranks as a 'first' for the

A typical specimen of the millions of egg-shaped bottles issued for most of the nineteenth century. They were embossed: 'J. SCHWEPPE & CO./51 BERNERS STREET/OXFORD STREET/GENUINE SUPERIOR/AERATED WATERS'

company. Jacob Schweppe retired in 1798 and returned to Geneva, where he died in November 1821.

At the close of 1831 the company moved to its famous address, 51 Berners Street – an address that appeared on millions of egg-shaped bottles. At that same period they became 'Soda and Mineral Water Manufacturers to Their Majesties and the Royal Family'.

In 1835, Schweppes Aerated Lemonade was introduced; it was not until 1931 that they introduced aerated orange drink! In 1837, two months after coming to the throne, Queen Victoria granted a new royal warrant of appointment to the firm as purveyors of soda water. The company is proud that succeeding monarchs have honoured them in the same way.

In the 1870s, tonic water and ginger ale were added to the range of products. In 1930 the company purchased a 51% interest in Kia-Ora Ltd, a company with Australasian roots. *Kia-Ora* is a Maori word meaning 'good health'.

For many years Schweppes has been well-known for its advertisements. These became particularly innovative in the late 1940s and early 1950s under Stephen Potter and Sir Frederic Hooper. Such words as Schweppshire, Schwepsom Downs, Schweppervescence and Schwepping days were coined. They still live on today.

Schweppes advertising continued to be in the spotlight with the birth of perhaps the most famous of all the Schweppes advertising campaigns – 'The secret of Schh . . . you-know-who' starring William Franklyn. It kept the Schweppes name in the public eye and created a famous catchphrase.

In 1969, Schweppes merged with the Cadbury Group to become Cadbury Schweppes. Expansion followed and, by 1989, Schweppes drinks were on sale in 52 countries worldwide.

All the latest developments in the imaginary English county of Schweppshire could be found in its own newspaper

One of a series of three paintings by Maynard Brown, c1900, for Schweppes advertising

The slogan 'Schweppervescence' was introduced to the public in June 1946 – but after its withdrawal during the war, the brand itself did not reappear until February 1948! This advert appeared in 1949

Schweppervescence
lasts the whole drink through

Silver Cross

When William Wilson was only twenty-one years old, he moved from Sunderland to Leeds to work as a perambulator spring-smith. Some years later, in 1877, he started his own business as a pram manufacturer in small premises in Hunslet, Leeds.

A prolific inventor, William held more than thirty patents – they included patents for an improved double suspension hammock, folding shafts for mail carts and also a convertible mailcart. All these various inventions led to a continuous and steady growth of the business.

The 'Baby Carriage' of 1887

The original factory was in Silver Cross Street, Leeds. In 1898 a new factory was built in White-house Street, but a year later this was

William Wilson was a prolific inventor

destroyed by fire. In 1936 the company made its final move to its present headquarters and works in Guiseley, a few miles from Leeds.

During the Second World War, Wilsons found themselves involved in working to aid the war effort. Their involvement in new techniques for the manipulation of aluminium for aircraft parts led to them developing a new method of manufacturing baby carriages. As the years have passed, many other new processes have been developed to ensure that Wilsons perambulators have continued to be a top quality product.

For many years a Rolls Royce appeared in their advertisements. Mr Lawrence Wilson, William's grandson, who served the company for fifty years, said:

'Rolls Royce engines are the acme of engineering. It is my aim that our products shall be synonymous with the very best, the finest there is amongst baby carriages.'

To mark the creation of a most ambitious and expensive range of luxury baby carriages, the trade name Wilson was added to the now famous Silver Cross brand in 1957. The Wilson brand name remained strong until being discontinued in 1976, keeping only the original brand name of Silver Cross. The company also

changed its name to Silver Cross Limited in 1988.

Each year, 124,000 baby carriages of all types are produced at Guiseley, many of these being exported to countries around the world.

'The World's Most Exclusive Baby Coach'
in the 1950s

Albert Slazenger

Mordecai Slazenger settled in the north of England, and in 1800 was an umbrella maker in Manchester, although later he owned a string of tailor's shops. Slazenger is an anglicised version of Schlesinger, which meant 'from Silesia', now part of Poland. However, the family believe they originated from Scandinavia and it is possible they came from a Swedish or Danish port. It is also believed that, not wishing to risk any anti-semitic reaction, they adopted the most common name in use in Manchester, Moss. In trade directories they used the name Slazenger Moss. Mordecai Slazenger died in 1819.

It was two of his grandchildren, Albert and Ralph Slazenger (Moss), who were to start the long association with the game of lawn tennis, a game invented in 1873 by Major Walter Clopton Wingfield who named it 'Sphairistike'! In 1881, Slazengers sold 'The New Game of Lawn Tennis' complete in a box.

In 1877, at 23 Market Street, Manchester, was 'Slazenger et Fils, importer of French fancy goods'. In 1881 this company was registered as gaiter and legging manufacturers at 14, 16 and 18 Corporation Street, with factories in Manchester and Paris. This was in effect the founding of Slazengers as we know it today. In 1885 they moved their business to 56 Cannon Street, in London, and Ralph officially changed his name from Moss to Slazenger. They advertised themselves as india rubber goods manufacturers, until 1890 when the Post Office directory of London describes them as 'Slazenger and Sons, india rubber goods manufacturers, waterproofers, lawn tennis rackets and appliances and cricket bat makers, football and football boots, legging and gaiter manufacturer'.

Slazengers first started to manufacture lawn tennis rackets in 1881 and lawn tennis balls a few years later. Ever since, they have been used by the world's greatest players and in all countries around the world. Every year since 1902 the Slazenger tennis ball has been used at Wimbledon.

In 1953 the company was taken over by the Dunlop Corporation, thus severing a seventy-two year long family link. Today Dunlop Slazenger International Ltd is part of BTR, one of Britain's largest and most successful conglomerates.

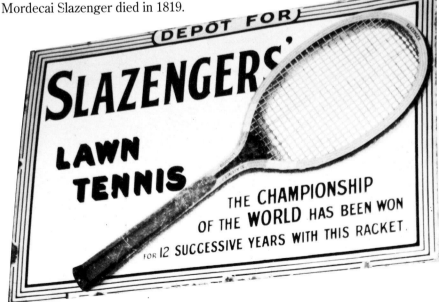

(DEPOT FOR)
SLAZENGERS'
LAWN TENNIS
THE CHAMPIONSHIP OF THE WORLD HAS BEEN WON FOR 12 SUCCESSIVE YEARS WITH THIS RACKET

Tom Smith

Just when Tom Smith, a London baker and confectioner, had his brilliant idea is not known, but it must have been in the years immediately prior to 1847, the date he founded his company. The idea of the cracker appears, like so many novelties, to have come in a roundabout way.

He started his own business from premises in Goswell Road in East London, making wedding cake ornaments and other confectionery. In his search for new ideas Tom Smith travelled abroad, on one trip going to Paris where he stumbled across the bonbon. A French confectioner had conceived the idea of wrapping some of his sweets in tissue paper. On returning to England a few weeks before Christmas, he purchased a stock of tissue paper and sugared almonds, thus making the first supply of bonbons ever sold in England.

After the Christmas season the sale of bonbons ceased. With much thought he came up with the idea of placing a small love motto inside the bonbon wrapping. His customers agreed to take supplies, but somehow he had to

Some examples of late nineteenth century crackers

find a way to make the bonbons more of a novelty for the short Christmas season.

The story goes that he was thinking about this one Christmas while standing in front of a smouldering log fire. The Yule log had long been part of the Christmas tradition and its appeal was, thought Tom, that it blazed up suddenly with a jolly crackle and shower of sparks when given a good kick.

He could make a paper log which concealed items such as a toy, a sweet and a motto. That part was easy but he wanted it to open with a bang. It took two years to develop a commercially successful 'bang'. It was now only a matter of chemical experimentation to find a combination which was satisfactory. Initially he produced his own 'snaps' but these were later obtained from outside suppliers. The first crackers were called 'coasques'.

Tom Smith began to explore the export market, but as a result an Eastern manufacturer copied the idea

and dumped a consignment in this country. Although the rival supplies only arrived just before Christmas he immediately designed eight different kinds, and, working his staff day and night, soon had stocks all over the country in time for the festive season.

Late in the 1920s the company produced a cracker larger than anything previously made – it was eighteen feet long, and when pulled at a banquet in London, waitresses walked from inside the cracker and distributed gifts.

Today Tom Smith employ over 400 people and produce over 50 million crackers each year, many of these being exported to the 50 different countries where crackers are enjoyed whenever there is an occasion to celebrate. The company also makes indoor fireworks, balloons, party poppers, hats and other seasonal novelties.

Tom Smith's idea for Christmas crackers was inspired by a flaming Yule log

The 1910 catalogue of 'Christmas Novelties'

⦀SMITHS≡

In the early 1900s, Frank Smith was manager of Carters, a wholesale grocery company in the City of London. In 1910 Mr Carter, the company's proprietor, brought from abroad a recipe for a French speciality table dish – thinly-sliced potatoes cooked in oil.

The idea of making and selling these appealed to Frank Smith. The two men, after experimenting with hand-cutting equipment to get potato slices of uniform thickness, decided to market the product, 'potato crisps', in 2d bags. Distribution was by horse-drawn vehicles and was very local. The idea did not show any signs of growth, as neither the trade nor the public really knew what a potato crisp was.

Mr Carter was not wildly enthusiastic, but Frank Smith saw great possibilities in the product. In 1920 he branched out on his own, with £10,000 capital subscribed by himself and two friends. He formed Smiths Potato Crisps Ltd.

A staff of twelve began work in a converted store behind the Crown Hotel, Cricklewood. This time the business did grow rapidly, and even the London sales overtook production. By 1921, other factories were opened to cope with the demand.

In 1922 came the addition of the now-famous salt packet – salt wrapped in a blue paper twist. This quickly became the Smiths trademark.

Up until 1939, production was almost entirely on a manual basis. A gas-fired furnace heated a large tank of ground nut oil. A cook cut potato slices, cooked them in oil, draining them ready for packing. In the 1950s, with automation came greater expansion. In 1961, Smiths Potato Crisps Ltd took over other competitors, producing not only crisps but also nuts and biscuits.

Also during this period, the product itself was developed and flavoured crisps were introduced. Their arrival brought quite a boost in sales.

In 1968, General Mills Inc, a large American food organisation, acquired total control. Smiths Potato Crisps Ltd became the Smiths Food Group.

Today, at their ten factories in the UK, automatic cookers taking 6,000lb of potatoes hourly, produce about 1,400lb of finished crisps per hour.

Above *Delivery – 1920s style*

Hand packing crisps in the late 1920s

From early days, Smiths crisps were promoted as good for you

SMITH'S POTATO CRISPS

MEDICAL OPINION *says*

"SIX TIMES THE FOOD VALUE OF BOILED POTATOES"

All Vitamins Retained

This is because Smith's Crisps are cooked in pure vegetable oil, by a process which not only prevents the nutritive losses caused by ordinary cooking, but also breaks down the starch, thus rendering the crisps easily digestible and non-fattening.

THEY ARE DELICIOUS TO EAT
THEY ARE CHEAP

2d., 3d. and 6d. per packet.
Family Tins 7½d. and 1/4d.

Worth their salt!

SMITH'S POTATO CRISPS (1929) LTD., GREAT WEST ROAD, BRENTFORD, MIDDLESEX

Smith ✚ Nephew

In Hull in 1856, Thomas James Smith opened his chemist's shop, describing himself as an 'Analytical & Pharmaceutical Chemist'. He probably never dreamed that from such small a beginning would grow one of the world's largest surgical dressings companies.

He was an enterprising young man, thirty years old, and extremely interested in medicine and also a member of the newly-formed British Pharmaceutical Society. His interests eventually led him to turn from the retail pharmacy to become a wholesale supplier to hospitals. One of his first projects was the supply of cod liver oil, widely prescribed at the time.

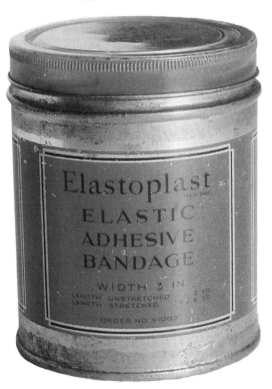

It was not until 1896 that the nephew, Horatio Nelson Smith, joined his uncle. Horatio had started working for a wholesale draper and woollen manufacturer in London. It was there that he acquired his knowledge of textile manufacture. His uncle was beginning to suffer ill-health and his sister, Amelia Ann Smith, wrote to Horatio asking him to join his uncle. In July 1896, T J Smith issued a notice of partnership formally founding the company under the name of T J Smith and Nephew.

Thomas Smith (left) *and his nephew Horatio*

Three months later Thomas James Smith died, leaving his half of the business to Amelia Ann. However, a few years later she decided to transfer this share to Horatio, together with all the furniture in the house, in exchange for an annuity of £260 a year during her lifetime. This odd transaction was not witnessed by a lawyer but by the family doctor. It gave Horatio full control of a thriving business.

His training in textiles was now to begin to make its mark on the company. A machine for cutting and rolling bandages was bought from Germany, the cloth being purchased from Lancashire.

In 1907 the firm became a limited company. The same year the company moved to a larger building, 5 Neptune Street. Today the company occupies both sides of the whole length of Neptune Street and is still expanding.

1928 was a turning point in the company's history. The 'Elastoplast' elastic adhesive bandage was developed and soon revolutionised the treatment of varicose ulcers. Today Elastoplast is often regarded as a generic term for sticking plasters, but is, in fact, a trade mark of Smith & Nephew. In other countries it is sold under the name of Tensoplast.

In 1951, Herts Pharmaceuticals was acquired. This not only brought pharmaceutical products such as Nivea cream, but also laboratories and staff which provided the basis of the Smith & Nephew Research Company.

Today the medical side of the business is still controlled from Hull by Smith and Nephew Medical Ltd, but there are many other companies within the Smith and Nephew Group, marketing such brands as Nivea, Atrixo, Lilia, Tender Touch, Minims and Welldorm. There are Smith and Nephew companies, branches and agencies in all the major countries of the world. In 1989 there were over 14,400 employees worldwide.

In 1564 a deposit of graphite was found in a form so solid and uniform that it could be sawn into sheets, and then into leads. This find, in the Lake District, was so valuable that armed guards escorted the wagons to London.

In Nürnberg, Germany, as early as 1662, Friedrich Staedtler was mentioned as a 'pencil maker'. Throughout the generations the family continued to make pencils. The Lakeland graphite mines were soon exhausted and so Friedrich's great grandson, Paulus Staedtler, started experimenting with the new process invented in 1785: clay was mixed with ground graphite and then fired to form a solid lead.

The factory, which had been moved outside the Nürnberg city walls to the present location of Johannis, had grown to some size by the beginning of the twentieth century. Several of these buildings still stand today

The old production methods were discarded and new 'industrialised' pencil manufacture began.

In 1835, Johann Sebastian Staedtler founded the company and, firstly using water power and later a small steam engine, became independent of the family business. This involved establishing a factory with lead mills, cutting, slotting and shaping machines, and kilns – and a lot of capital and a considerable amount of courage. In 1840 at the Nürnberg Industrial Exhibition, the company exhibited sixty-three different types of pencils.

Around 1870, J S Staedtler retired and was followed into the business by his three sons. At this time the annual production was about two million pencils and sales extended to Austria, France, Great Britain, Italy, Russia and the Orient. Even then they had representatives working on a commission basis travelling the globe. The 1870s brought financial difficulties, and over a period of years it passed into the hands of the Kreutzer brothers. They

rebuilt the company's fortunes but again it had to be rebuilt from scratch after the First World War. By 1920 they were producing 33 million pencils a year.

The production of graphite at the Staedtler factory in 1912

Staedtler's trademark at this time was a personified half moon, registered in 1894. The Mars trademark, still recognised as a sign of quality today, was registered in 1900.

1949 saw the introduction of their ballpoint pen production. Other important developments have included the manufacture of drafting instruments of the highest precision, as well as inks and writing liquids.

Staedtler now exports to over 150 counties from manufacturing bases in eight countries. A stylised version of the Mars warrior's head now serves as the company trademark.

The half moon trademark (left) *was registered in 1894*

Below
A half gross box of early Mars pencils

Start-rite

James Smith set up as a shoemaker, making ladies shoes and selling leather, in the Upper Market in Norwich, near to the present City Hall in 1792. In 1816, James was succeeded by Charles Winter who imported machinery from America to sew the uppers, and later on other machines that would sew soles to the uppers. This was in about 1856.

1865 saw the business once again change hands, this time to be taken over by Messrs Willis and Southall. Until the end of the First World War the factory was still making ladies shoes, but soon after that the firm started making children's shoes. During the Second World War a Board of Trade directive instructed that 83% of production should be children's shoes. As a result, the company approached the subject with a great deal of care to ensure that their shoes best met the needs of children's growing feet, introducing footwear in up to five different fittings.

About the same time that James Smith was setting up his business in Norwich, Henry Quant was opening a shoe shop in Bury St Edmunds. During 1921, Quant and Son brought out a patent design for children's shoes and gave them the name Start-rite. As early as 1925, they had an X-ray machine in their shop to view how the child's foot was fitting within the shoe.

The patent for Start-rite was later sold to the Norwich company. For the next fifty years, Quants received a royalty of 3d per dozen pairs, up to a maximum of £500 per year.

The famous Start-rite twins originate from 1947, when the company's advertising agent was driving back to London from an appointment with the company in Norwich. At this meeting, he had been urged to think of something original to promote Start-rite children's shoes. As he drove down the straight tree-lined road between Newmarket and Cambridge, he was reminded of the illustration in Kipling's *Just So Stories* of 'The Cat that Walked by Himself', and he developed the idea into the original twins walking up the road to a lifetime's foot health. The painting for the advertisement was done by Mrs Susan Pearse. The twins'

poster was featured on the London Underground for well over twenty years, and the twins still appear on all Start-rite infants shoes.

The company is constantly reprimanded by children writing to complain that the twins should not be walking in the middle of the road. It explains that it must be a private road in a traffic-free park!

Kipling's story of 'The Cat that Walked by Himself' was the inspiration for the Start-rite twins

The Start-rite twins walking to a lifetime of foot health

Subbuteo®

Ever since soccer became organised into clubs and leagues, many attempts have been made to recreate the excitement of the real game on a table top. Nothing really caught on until 1947 when Peter Adolph launched Subbuteo in the UK. But why the name Subbuteo ? Adolph wanted to call it the Hobby (after the hobby hawk) but he was not allowed to register that name, so he took the Latin name for hawk, *Falco subbuteo subbuteo*, the name eventually becoming just Subbuteo.

Peter Adolph at a recent Earls Court Toy Fair, where Subbuteo was given the British Association of Toy Retailers award of 'Top Action Game for over 40 Years'

Early dispatches went out from a former hayloft over some stables; they included within their instruction details, 'Mark your pitch on an ex-Army blanket'. It was not until the early 1950s that a well marked-out playing cloth was produced.

The original 'Assembly' edition cost 10s 6d, and comprised cardboard teams, paper 'netting' for metal-framed do-it-yourself goals, and celluloid balls. Soon improvements followed – assembled goals, real netting, a panelled ball, additional teams and a green cloth on which the pitch could be marked with chalk. In the mid-1950s more accessories were

The original 'Assembly' edition (below) had cut-out cardboard teams and no pitch

Left *By 1950, the game came with its own pitch*

Below left *The 1984 Subbuteo senior world championship*

introduced, including referees, linesmen, white and orange coloured panelled balls, even a score recorder.

Later still came the C100 type '00' scale, with hand-painted figures. Subbuteo cricket and rugby were also introduced. Table Soccer Players' Associations have been formed, and in 1970 a world cup tournament was launched. The winners were West Germany, who beat Belgium 2–0.

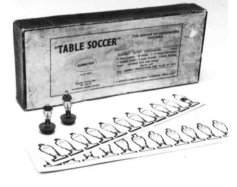

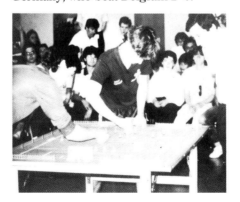

These all provide opportunity for those who play the game to enjoy a sense of real competition, as they might do in full-size soccer. Entrants from over twenty nations now compete in the 'world cup', and over 300 different team strips are now available.

Subbuteo is now owned by Waddingtons.

SWAN

The earliest electric kettles had their elements underneath the kettle, rather than within it. Swan was the first company to manufacture a kettle where it was inside with the water – at first people were terrified at the idea of mixing water and electricity. This kettle was developed by Leslie Large, who worked as an electrical engineer for Bulpitt & Sons Ltd in Birmingham. At this time they made 'Swan' products, a name derived from Swansea Tin Plate. At first it was known as a 'patent electric cooking utensil', but the idea caught on. It cost

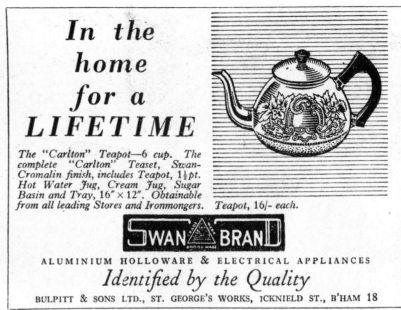

In the home for a LIFETIME

The "Carlton" Teapot—6 cup. The complete "Carlton" Teaset, Swan-Cromalin finish, includes Teapot, 1½ pt. Hot Water Jug, Cream Jug, Sugar Basin and Tray, 16″ × 12″. Obtainable from all leading Stores and Ironmongers. Teapot, 16/- each.

SWAN BRAND

ALUMINIUM HOLLOWARE & ELECTRICAL APPLIANCES
Identified by the Quality
BULPITT & SONS LTD., ST. GEORGE'S WORKS, ICKNIELD ST., B'HAM 18

M-W.144

18s 6d in 1935, or 22s with a patent automatic safety device. In 1937 an ejector was introduced, which disconnected the kettle from the electricity supply if the kettle was allowed to boil dry.

1939 saw a move to bring design and fashion into the kitchen. By using stainless steel, it was possible to develop a kettle 'in keeping with the best table silver'.

Above *A 1949 advert*

Left *An early Swan kettle from the 1920s*

It was not until 1975 that a fully automatic kettle was introduced – the Swan Automatic – which switched itself off automatically when the water boiled, and which had a reset button which could be pressed to bring the water back to the boil.

Whilst initially the idea of the jug kettle was started in the 1960s by Swan, it is only in recent years that the concept has become so popular. This has been followed by the cordless jug kettle, eliminating the hazard of the trailing lead.

TATE+LYLE

Sir Henry Tate (left) *and Abram Lyle*

Henry Tate, the son of a Lancashire clergyman, had moved to Liverpool when he was thirteen years old. He became an apprentice to a grocer and when he was twenty years old he started his own business. By 1855 he owned six very successful shops, but his interest in sugar refining was such that he severed his connection with the grocery shops and sold them.

In 1859 he became a partner in a sugar refining company; in 1869 he bought it and changed its name to Henry Tate & Sons. They constructed a sugar refinery in Love Lane, Liverpool, and this was opened in 1872. They then extended their activities to London, mainly for the refining of cane sugar.

Henry Tate was a very generous man. He is best remembered as the founder of the National Gallery of British Art – the Tate Gallery – which was opened in 1897.

Abram Lyle became interested in sugar refining in 1865 when, with a partner, he started the Glebe Sugar Refining Company in Greenock, Scotland. At that time Greenock was the leading port in the west of Scotland, and had become a great centre for the sugar industry. Abram's father was a ship owner, and Abram had been involved in bringing cargoes of raw sugar and mollasses from the West Indies.

In 1881 Lyles sold out their interest in the Glebe Refinery and moved to London. At Plaistow they obtained a wharf and a site, where in 1882 they completed the Plaistow Wharf Refinery, at which they were to specialise in their Golden Syrup.

The Tate and Lyle families now had

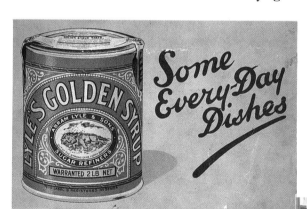

refineries within a mile of each other in the Silvertown area. They continued in active opposition until 1921, when Tate & Lyle was created by the amalgamation of the two companies. Between 1921 and 1945, the company expanded rapidly both at home and abroad.

Sugar bag filling in 1935 at the Tate & Lyle refinery

The symbol 'Mr Cube' came into existence in 1949 to fight the Government's nationalisation plans, and proved a great success.

Golden Syrup still bears the name 'Lyle's Golden Syrup' with its picture of the lion lying down surrounded by flying bees. Underneath is the phrase from the Bible, Book of Judges, ch 14 verse 14, referring to the story of Samson:

'Out of the strong came forth sweetness.'

Left   *An early book of recipes using Lyle's Golden Syrup*

Below   *Henry Tate's first grocery shop*

THERMOS

The first vacuum was produced in 1643 by Evangelista Torricelli, an Italian physicist and philosopher. Two hundred and fifty years later an English scientist, Sir James Dewar, experimenting with temperature retention in 1892, invented a special flask – one glass bottle sealed within another, and the air pumped out from between the two. These early flasks were extremely fragile and required careful handling. They were unsilvered, but later models contained a drop of mercury which condensed to form a mirror. It was not until Dewar sought a glass-blowing expert in Germany that the first successful vacuum flask was made for use in laboratories. Commercial manufacturing, to his design, began in 1898. It served its scientific purpose well but was of little value to the public.

The vacuum flask was never patented by Sir James Dewar. He gave his idea to the world of science without a thought as to its commercial possibilities, though he was fully aware that it could be used for keeping liquids hot, almost equally as well as for keeping them cold, which was what he required.

Dewar's German glass-blower, Reinhold Burger, was a partner in the firm of Burger and Aschenbrenner, manufacturers of scientific glass apparatus. While making the flasks for Dewar, they conceived the idea of a domestic vacuum flask with protective metal casing. A patent for this was secured in Germany in 1903.

A competition was organised for a name for the vacuum bottle, and a resident of Munich submitted the word 'Thermos', derived from the Greek word *therme*, meaning heat. The firm known as Thermos Gesellschaft MBH was formed in Berlin for the manufacturing of vacuum flasks. From March 1904 they called their product Thermos. Within a year it was also being sold in the USA.

Thermos Ltd was formed in the UK in 1907, and registered the brand name Thermos in the UK, the British Empire and many other parts of the world. In 1908, Thermos Ltd opened their first factory in Tottenham, London. In 1915, all links with the German company were severed.

Initially, each flask was individually blown – and cost a guinea. By 1911, mechanisation had reduced this to 2s 6d. The 1920s and 1930s saw a great demand for Thermos flasks, as people took them on picnics or to work. All production was given over to the armed forces during the Second World War, and every thousand bomber raid would mean around 12,000 Thermos flasks in the air as well.

In 1946, the first royal warrant was granted by King George VI. A new factory was opened at Brentwood in 1954, and all manufacturing was moved there in 1962.

Today, Thermos Ltd exports to around 100 countries, and assiduously protects its brand name and trademarks.

A 1909 advert extols the uses for the new Thermos flask

TOBLERONE®

Johann Jakob Tobler was born on the 17th March 1830 in Wienacht-Tobel, Switzerland. He was raised in a small farming community and became an apprentice confectioner when fourteen years old. For the next seventeen years he worked as a journeyman in France and Germany, gaining wide experience. He also changed his name to Jean.

When he returned to Switzerland in 1865, he settled first in Vevey. (It was here that Henri Nestlé started his chocolate firm.) In 1867 he moved to Berne, where he took over a famous confectionery business in one of the town's main streets. Initially all work was done manually, but in August 1899, work began in a small factory producing the first chocolate branded 'J Tobler'. Tobler died in 1905 and the firm was then run by his three children.

In 1908 the production manager Emil Baumann went to Metz to study confectionery production. He was so impressed with the Montelimar nougat he saw, that on his return he suggested to his cousin Theodor Tobler that it be combined with milk chocolate. That same evening they conducted a series of experiments in the kitchen, where Emil succeeded in combining Tobler milk chocolate with almonds and pure honey. Having visited Italy several times, Tobler noticed the Italian name for nougat: *torrone*. It seemed natural to combine this with the family name, and so the name of Toblerone was created. Having succeeded in producing a new chocolate, it was decided to give it a distinctive shape. The triangular bar with its handy serrations seemed the perfect solution, for not only did it seem to suggest the peaks of Swiss mountains but it allowed the bar to be easily broken into perfect bite-size pieces. The packaging, with its inscriptions, decorations and colours, has changed very little over the years.

Johann Tobler

To protect it from imitation, Toblerone was granted a patent in 1909. In 1970 the company merged with the Suchard group to form Jacob Suchard Tobler.

Toblerone is the best-known Swiss chocolate all over the world. The production is centralised in Berne, from where Toblerone goes to more than 110 countries. Jacob Suchard Tobler is the greatest exporter of Swiss chocolate, and every second tablet is Toblerone.

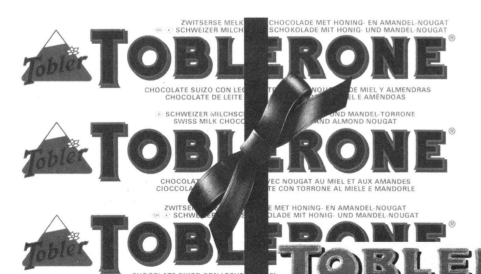

Right   *The Toblerone packaging hasn't changed much over the years, as this wrapper used between 1920–31 shows*

Tupperware®

Earl Silas Tupper came from a poor family in Berlin, New Hampshire, USA. He worked for the large Dupont chemical company, who were experimenting with plastics before the Second World War. He was also interested in experimenting with this new substance, but as he could not buy it he asked his bosses to sell him some of the left-over material. What they let him have was a chunk of polythene slag, a waste product of the oil refining process. It was black, rock hard, putrid and almost impossible to work with. However, he was not to be put off, and he developed a refining process to purify the slag and an injection-moulding machine to make his new products.

Not only did he find a practical way to make a new plastic that was tough, lightweight, flexible and non-breakable, but he also developed a practical application that took advantage of its characteristics. He saw his unbreakable food storage containers, plates, cups and bowls with their special qualities as a boon to busy mothers. So innovative were they that the American Museum of Modern Art has fifteen of the earliest designs in its permanent collection. It took him a little longer to invent the virtually airtight and liquid-tight Tupperware seal – he modelled it on the lid of a tin of paint, only in reverse!

In 1938 he founded the Tupperware Plastics Company, and in 1942 bought his first manufacturing plant, a factory in Farnumsville, Massachusetts. In 1945 he introduced Tupper Plastics brand products to the American consumer in hardware and department stores. They were displayed, and often stayed, on store shelves because no-one could work out how to operate the seal.

Sales took off after some direct sellers had demonstrated them. Tupper recognised this power of direct selling as sales

Earl Tupper first produced his food containers from a waste product of the oil refining process

rocketed, and in 1951 he took all his products off the store shelves. One of those first direct sellers was Brownie Wise, and Tupper hired her to create the direct selling system for Tupperware.

She knew how to put fun into the home party and also how to make a career exciting and enjoyable. It was Brownie who invented the sales promotions, contests and party games, not forgetting the support, training and recognition so necessary to motivate staff. This was a new way of work for many, where they could choose to work as much or as little as they wanted.

In 1960 this new concept was introduced into Great Britain. In the United Kingdom and Ireland there are now 10,000 demonstrators giving a total of 5,000 parties a week. In 1989 more than 88 million people attended a Tupperware party, and there are now dealers in 43 countries. Worldwide, a Tupperware party starts every 2.7 seconds!

TWININGS

Thomas Twining began selling tea in the early 1700s

Thomas Twining was brought to London in 1684 from Painswick in Gloucestershire by his father to take up an apprenticeship as a weaver, although it is probable that he never intended to become one. He was employed by Thomas D'Aeth of St Giles, a wealthy East India merchant, remaining with him until he was thirty-one years old.

In 1706, Thomas Twining acquired Tom's Coffee House in Devereaux Court, just off the Strand. At that time, coffee houses

The famous Twinings doorway at 216 Strand

were flourishing. As the competition was so keen, proprietors would introduce 'gimmicks' – his was the selling of tea as a sideline. By 1717, his business was expanding so much that he bought two small houses next door. As the premises had no numbers in those days, he chose the 'king of beasts' as his sign and clothed him in prophetic gold, hence the Golden Lion.

In 1784 Thomas's grandson, Richard, as chairman of the Dealers of Tea, persuaded William Pitt, the prime minister of the time, to reduce the high tax on tea, thus making Britain the tea-drinking nation it is today. He also built the famous doorway at 216 Strand, unveiled on the 10th April 1787; it was followed by a banking business in 1824, which was later moved to 215 Strand with a connecting door to the tea warehouse. In 1892, Twinings Bank was amalgamated with Lloyds Bank and moved to 222 Strand.

In 1837, the first year of Queen Victoria's reign, Twinings was granted a royal warrant 'as Purveyor of Tea in Ordinary to her Majesty' and has held royal warrants for every successive sovereign to this day.

Today the company has modern factories in Andover, Newcastle and Greensboro, USA; its head office also being in Andover. The famous shop still continues to trade at 216 Strand, but Twinings tea is also available in more than ninety countries.

Twinings remains the oldest tea company, and is the oldest company trading on the same site, with the same name and the same product for nearly 300 years – a unique record.

VICKS

Lunsford Richardson was born in 1854 and brought up on a farm in North Carolina. Times were hard, especially after the death of his father while

This puts a quick end to catarrh misery

When your nose is stuffy, your head dull and aching from catarrh, try this for quick and long-lasting relief: Melt a spoonful of " Vick " in a bowl or jug of boiling water, put a towel or paper around it in the form of a funnel and breathe deeply the powerful, medicated vapours for ten minutes. Your nose opens up at once, your whole head feels clear and cool. To keep breathing easy, put a little " Vick " up each nostril ; repeat as needed.

In tests by doctors among 17,353 people, " Vick " ended colds quicker. Insist on genuine " Vick." 1/3, or double quantity 2/-.

VICK BRAND VAPOUR-RUB

Lunsford was still a baby. It was a miracle that his mother managed to raise the few hundred dollars needed to send him to college. However, he rewarded her sacrifice by completing the four year course in only three years.

After college his first job was as a teacher, which he did not enjoy, and so he decided to change his career and become a pharmacist.

In 1890, along with his wife and family, he moved to a small market town, Greensboro, where, with a partner, he bought a drugstore. Many poor farmers who lived in the surrounding areas could not afford to consult doctors, and so they often asked him to prescribe medicine to cure their ailments.

As the years went by, so his range of home remedies expanded. He sold them under the name 'Vicks' – he had seen the name in a magazine for Vicks Seeds. He had wanted a name that was short and easily remembered. Vick was also the name of his brother-in-law.

Eventually the 'Vicks Family Remedies' reached twenty-one in number. However, it was the vapourising salve he had produced to cure colds which was to become important. It was known later as Vicks VapoRub, but had initially been produced to relieve the 'croup' of his eldest child. He had included menthol, at that time

An advert from 1939

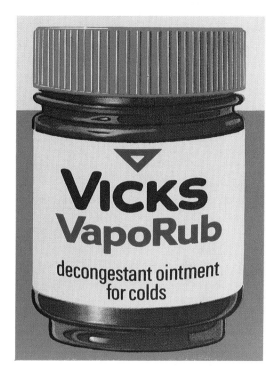

a new drug from Japan, into an ointment base together with rubefacient ingredients. When the ointment was rubbed on a person's chest, the heat of the body vapourised the menthol, permitting the soothing medicated vapours to be inhaled for hours. As there was no internal medication there was no danger of stomach upset, but the rubefacient ingredients had the effect of a hot poultice.

Today the famous product still relieves the suffering of many people, the name of Richardson being remembered in the manufacturer's name, Richardson-Vicks, now part of the Proctor and Gamble Company.

Wall's traces its beginnings back to the year 1786, when young Richard Wall was apprenticed to a meat and pie business in St James' Market in central London. In 1806 he took over ownership, and as trade grew so he moved the family firm to larger premises in nearby Jermyn Street.

Thomas Wall, the grandson of Richard, was born in 1846. By the time he took control of the business, daily deliveries of pies and sausages to royal palaces in the city had become well-established.

Thomas Wall, the last of the family dynasty

At this time, commercial refrigeration was still in its infancy. People held a superstition that you should not eat pork if there was not an 'R' in the month – May, June, July, and August – the warm months of the year. This hit meat and particularly pie sales at this time of the year.

It is said that a young clerk working in the offices at Poole first suggested the idea of making ice cream in 1913, but nothing was done about it due to the onset of the First World War.

When the subject was revived in 1922, Wall's had already moved to a six acre site at Acton. About this time, William Hesketh Lever established a chain of fish shops – MacFisheries – across the country. Eventually he felt a need to sell meat pies and sausages through his shops, and approached Wall's for supplies. When Wall's did introduce ice cream that year, their aim was to sell it through these outlets that they had already supplied – the butchers and fishmongers – but they did not want to be bothered with ice cream.

However, Wall's now had six operatives making ice cream, about 150 gallons a week, all in the form of hand-wrapped briquettes. It was Tom's brother, Fred, who came up with the winning idea:

'Why not buy a trike?'

The suggestion did not gain favour, but one was bought for £6, loaded with ice and ice cream briquettes, and it set off around the streets of Acton. The memorable date was the 16th July 1922. There was nothing on the trike to display its

Wall's developed ice cream in the early 1920s – and 'Stop me and Buy One' became a national institution

wares, but its rider had a good voice and such good sales were made that nine more tricycles were bought ready for next year.

Thomas Wall died in 1930.

The slogan 'Stop me and Buy one' became a household phrase, and by 1939 there were 8,500 trikes in operation from 136 depots. February 1959 saw the commencement, at

Gloucester, of what was to be the largest and most modern ice cream factory in the world – it is still so today.

In 1981, Wall's Ice Cream and Birds Eye merged to form Birds Eye Wall's, a company deeply involved in all aspects of the frozen food industry, employing over 5,000 people in highly-mechanised plants.

Wall's in the mid-1950s

WATERMAN

Lewis Edison Waterman, the founder of the Waterman Pen Company, in 1883

Lewis Edson Waterman, a forty-five year old insurance broker in New York, was getting ready to sign an important contract on a building site. He bought a new fountain pen for the occasion, thinking it would be more stylish and convenient than the usual dip pen (although he did have a pocket inkwell!). The contract was on the table and the client had the pen in his hand. Once, twice and even a third time the pen refused to write; even worse than that, it made a blot on the important document. Lewis rushed back to his office for another contract, but when he returned a rival broker had beaten him and signed another contract.

Waterman was determined to have his revenge – he invented his own fountain pen and started making them in his brother's workshop. He used the principle of capillarity, thus allowing air to replace ink, giving a smooth and steady flow. He baptised it the 'Regular'. It was long, decorated with wood, and was filled by using an eyedropper.

The following year, 1884, he obtained a patent for his pen. He intended making his fountain pens, but also continued to sell insurance. He opened a workshop at the back of a cigar shop and put up a sign:

'Waterman's Ideal Fountain Pen, guaranteed for five years.'

During that year he made, by hand, 500 fountain pens which had a thick, hard rubber barrel and wooden decorations. He advertised in a new magazine called *The Review of Review*. The orders poured in.

An agreement was signed with a New York company that made gold nibs; such was their faith in him they gave him his first dozen nibs! Variations of design and size were soon to follow, and in 1899 he was offering an extra-large 14 carat gold nib.

The following year a factory was set up in Montreal. Waterman published a pamphlet full of humour and sensible advice called the *Pen Prophet*. In it he announced the completion of a machine of five pens to sign five cheques simultaneously.

Lewis Waterman died in 1901, being succeeded by his nephew, Frank D Waterman. He crossed the Atlantic, to conquer, and raised sales figures to 350,000 pens a year. 1904 saw the introduction of special jewellery designs, and the development of what was then an exclusive feature – the cap with the clip – came in 1905.

At the beginning of the First World War, Jules Fagard took over the rights for France – after the war Lloyd George signed the Versailles Treaty with an extraordinary solid gold Waterman pen. Later Jules Fagard created his own company and Jif-Waterman was born. One of their research workers invented the nib cartridge, consisting of a small glass tube with a cork stopper. It was patented in 1935 and remained a Jif-Waterman exclusive for twenty years. Their pens became even more beautiful, being decorated with a diamond, bands of flowers in gold and silver, or having a miniature watch or telescope added!

After the Second World War, new developments were taking place in France, particularly the move towards a more general use of ball point pens, including the Pantabille with four interchangeable colours.

1954 saw the close-down of the American manufacturing facility, and Jif-Waterman became the largest of the companies trading with the Waterman trademark.

Today, after over a century of writing, Waterman pens are sold in 100 countries throughout the world. It is the largest manufacturer of writing instruments in Europe and the second largest world-wide.

An early advert for the Ideal fountain pen

WINSOR & NEWTON

In their business partnership, William Winsor (left) *was the artist and Henry Newton provided the scientific knowledge*

William Winsor and Henry C Newton were both in their late twenties, sharing an interest in painting. Newton was the more artistically gifted of the two whereas Winsor, who also painted, contributed the scientific knowledge that was to be so important. They established the firm at 38 Rathbone Place, London, in 1832. At that time a number of eminent painters, including Constable, had studios in the area, and other colourmen were already established.

The improvement of artists' watercolours was the partners' first concern. In the early 1800s, watercolours were sold in oblong cakes that had to be rubbed down with water on a surface such as ground glass, before the colour could be used. The two men utilised the moisture-retaining properties of glycerine to manufacture watercolours in pans that were much simpler and more convenient to use than watercolour cakes. In 1837 they introduced Chinese White paint, which was of considerable value to painters in watercolours. They were appointed artists' colourmen to Queen Victoria in 1841.

In 1844 the two men constructed a purpose-built, steam-powered factory at Kentish Town, known as the North London Colour Works.

In 1893 the firm gained three awards at the World's Columbian Exposition in Chicago, and the following year the firm set up an office in New York.

In 1915 an American subsidiary company was incorporated.

The Scholastic ranges were introduced in 1933. Today Winsor & Newton's colours, brushes, canvasses and easels are manufactured entirely at Wealdstone and Lowestoft, and are distributed through subsidiaries and agents throughout the world.

Winsor & Newton's watercolour room at the Colour Works in 1889. Colours were ground by hand and spread out onto stone slabs for partial drying. The screw presses on the right were used for forming artists' watercolour cakes

WISDOM®

Addis is one of the few businesses that was founded in the reign of King George III and is still in existence today.

William Addis was born in 1734, and opened his own business in 1780 in Whitechapel High Street, East London. He was described as being a stationer and rag merchant. During that same year he conceived the idea of a toothbrush for his personal use. He at once became aware of the commercial potential of his invention, and set about the manufacture and marketing of it. Those first tooth-brushes were made of bone and horse-hair.

His idea was imitated both in this country and in America. As his sons entered the business so it became known as William Addis & Son. He had started a new industry.

Hand-shaping bone toothbrushes in the 1920s

When William's son (also William) was twenty-one years old, his father died. Young William was already a skilled brush-maker, and he took control of the business. By about 1845 it was employing about sixty people, most of them being women who worked in their own homes. At that time there were fifty-three different processes involved in the making of an Addis toothbrush, most of them concerned with the shaping of the handle. Thigh and buttock bones from the ox, which had been boiled to remove fat and grease, were used to make the backs and handles. The working of the bones, including drilling holes to take the hairs, was a very delicate task. At this time the average price of these handmade brushes was 6d each.

In 1869, Addis advertised that their brushes were 'made by machinery', although at this time the filling of the holes was still done by hand.

By 1900 the importance of dental hygiene was growing, and by 1914 the firm was exporting toothbrushes throughout most parts of the world. In 1920 the firm moved to a five acre site in Hertford.

In 1923 the firm received its most demanding request, to make tooth

brushes for the famous Queen Mary's dolls house. The brushes, only three-quarters of an inch long, were made of ivory and hand-drawn with special silvered wire. The hair used was that taken from inside the ear of a goat, the finest white hair available.

Until 1926 most of the toothbrush handles were made from selected ox

Miniature brushes made for Queen Mary's dolls house, shown against an old 5p coin for comparison

bones, but in 1927 the firm started the manufacture of machine-filled plastic-handled toothbrushes.

In 1938 the company decided that it should launch a brand of its own to sell nationally. A completely new brush was designed, with a distinc-tively cranked plastic handle, a head trimmed flat along its length but curved across its width, and filled with the new nylon filaments from ICI.

The introduction of the new toothbrush was entrusted to an advertising agency, Graham & Gillies – they suggested that the new product be named Wisdom. Since that time, the name Wisdom has only been applied to toothbrushes and dental products.

The brush was an immediate success, even though at that time it sold at 2s and was slightly more expensive than the average toothbrush. Before long the Wisdom toothbrush was leading the market and the company was not able to satisfy the demand.

In 1947 the production of bone brushes was discontinued, bringing to an end 167 years of continuous work since William Addis' amazing prototype had been introduced.

In the 1950s the company was determined that it should increase its share of the market. It decided that it would endeavour to make the ideal toothbrush – to do so it enlisted the help of 14,000 dentists, asking them about handle length and shape, and type and composition of filling. The analysis of these replies helped the company to design the Wisdom Multituft.

Today Addis produces over 40 million toothbrushes each year.

Right   *Some unusual nineteenth century toothbrushes*

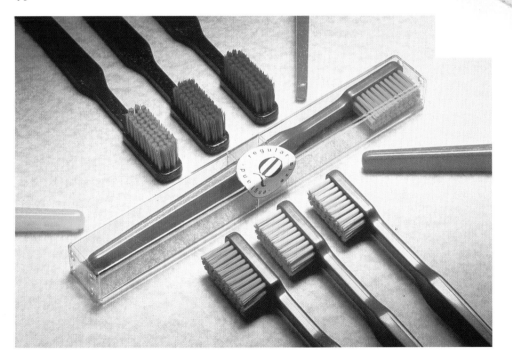

WRIGLEY'S

In 1891, William Wrigley moved from Philadelphia to Chicago, He was twenty-nine years old, had $32, and the ambition to start his own business. He also had a great talent as a salesman.

In his new business in Chicago, William sold soap to the wholesale trade. To stimulate buying, he offered various premiums with each purchase. One of the premiums, or free gifts, was baking powder. It proved to be more popular than the soap, so he decided to switch to the baking powder business. Then, one day in 1892, he had the idea of offering two packs of chewing gum with each can of baking powder. The offer was a big success. This time it was the chewing gum which seemed more promising.

William Wrigley began by selling soap, then baking powder – and finally chewing gum

Mr Wrigley decided that chewing gum was the product with the kind of future possibilities that he had been looking for. His first two brands of gum were named Lotta Gum and Vassar. Juicy Fruit came next in 1893, and Wrigley's Spearmint was introduced later in the same year.

He was a pioneer in the use of advertising to promote the sale of branded goods. He concentrated on his Spearmint, and in 1906 decided to advertise the gum on a modest scale. Results were promising and he made plans to expand it in 1907. That year a general business slump started and all companies slashed expenses. Not so Wrigley; he felt that with everyone else cutting back, this was the ideal time to get extra attention from his advertising.

By 1910, Wrigley's Spearmint was America's favourite gum. PK Chewing Gum – a sugar-coated gum in pellet form – was introduced in a tightly-sealed package rather than loose in a box. The product's name came from a slogan playing up

this feature: 'Packed tight – Kept right'.

Factories were established in Australia in 1915 and in Great Britain in 1927.

During the Second World War the armed forces took large quantities, as gum had proved a help to easing their tension, promoting alertness and improving morale. In 1944 the entire output was turned over to the US Armed Forces overseas and at sea. 'Got any gum, chum?' was a popular catchphrase of the time.

Today, the company has operations worldwide, with sales of $1 billion annually and is a market leader in many of the countries where the brands are sold.

A shop display aid from 1927

Yale

At the London Exhibition in 1851, an American lockmaker named Hobbs announced that he could pick any of the English-made locks. To the great astonishment of the makers, he picked them all, one after another. The

The first Yale keys (right) *did not have the grooves of a later model* (centre)*; and a modern key* (left)

English, however, were unable to pick Hobbs' own lock, but it was so complicated and expensive that its use was impractical, except in banks.

The display received great publicity, and other locksmiths attempted to improve existing locks to allay the anxiety of the public. The Infallible Bank Lock and the Magic Bank Lock appeared soon afterwards – the names alone were intended to inspire confidence in them. The inventor of these two locks was a brilliant young American locksmith, Linus Yale Jr. He was the son of one of America's leading bank lock manufacturers. Born in 1821 in Philadelphia, he was

originally a portrait painter, but soon acquired the family fascination with locks.

In 1844 his father, Linus Yale Sr, had patented a lock which was outside his main line of business. It was improved and perfected by his son, and with certain modifications, is the one which has become famous throughout the world as the Yale Cylinder Lock.

It employed the pin tumbler principle of the old, almost forgotten Egyptian lock and its Roman successor. When a key is inserted, its point passes under the pins and raises them so that they rest on top of the key bitings. The correct key lifts each pin to a point where the joint between the pin and its driver corresponds exactly with the joint between the plug and the cylinder. The plug is now free to rotate within the cylinder, the pins travelling with the plug and the drivers remaining stationary in their respective chambers. An incorrect key will not lift the pins to the correct height, and either the pin or the driver will be across the joint line, preventing the plug from turning.

Its important features are its security, adaptability and the smallness of the key. It paved the way for the mass

production of high-quality locks with the opportunity for the making of master keys. All the parts could be mass produced, but the end product was very difficult to pick.

Yale patented his lock in 1861 and 1865, and sales soon soared. In 1868, he formed a partnership with Henry R Towne to exploit the cylinder lock, and founded the Yale Lock Manufacturing Company in Stamford, Connecticut. Yale died that same year.

Today, Yale Security Products Ltd still focuses its mainstream business around the basic 5-pin tumbler lock, with its 24,000 possible key variations – virtually the same as Linus Yale's original design.

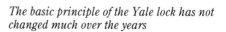

The basic principle of the Yale lock has not changed much over the years

It was in Kenosha, USA, that under-wear manufacturers Coopers Inc took the first step away from long johns and other unflattering underwear. They developed a garment where two flaps of the body fabric lapped over one another in an X formation, these overlaps being easily drawn aside and replaced – it was called the Kenosha Klosed Krotch. In 1911 it was the first item of male underwear to be nationally advertised, and sales boomed.

1934 saw the next milestone in the development of this now familiar garment. A senior vice-president of Coopers, idly glancing through a magazine, was intrigued by a pair of swimming trunks worn by one of the bathers on the French Riviera. The trunks had a stitched, slightly cupped, front section which offered the man a comfortable sustained control. It was the birth of the modern underpant.

The first experimental Y-Front was produced by Coopers under the factory name of Brief Style 1001 in September 1934, and received a US patent in August 1935. In knitted fabric with elastic waistband and a unique inverted Y-opening which left no gap, the Jockey Y-Front was

initially laughed to scorn by the rest of the industry.

A 'launch' window display had been booked for the large Marshall Field store in Chicago, but the city was having one of its winter blizzards. The drifting snow outside an exhibition of brief underclothing made it seem a nonsense, and the store management issued orders for the display to be changed and the cancel-lation of the advertise-ments. However the weather delayed the display men and someone forgot to cancel the advertise-ment. The 50 dozen stock sold out before noon! In the next eight day selling period, over 1,000 dozen pairs of Y-Fronts were sold.

In Britain, Charlie Oliver, managing director of Lyle and Scott, had been impressed by a pair of Y-Fronts he had seen, by chance, in the window of Simpsons of Piccadilly. This was 1938. He took a pair home, tried them on, and liked them.

During that same year an agreement was signed between Lyle and Scott and Coopers for the franchise for the UK, French and Danish markets. The agreement was for the production of Y-Front underpants in cotton to be made in Hawick. In Hawick, the holy of holies of the hosiery trade, many predicted the collapse of Lyle and Scott, but Y-Fronts were

different and comfortable – no buttons, no loops, no gaps!

During the war years, when salvage of rubber was important, they advertised:

'As a Y-Front wearer may we ask you, in the National interest, to return elastic bands from your old Y-Fronts to your Y-Front retailer . . .'

After the war Charlie Oliver, in bowler hat and with rolled umbrella, travelled the world opening up export markets. The advent of Jockeys or Boxers only helped to increase sales, and demand constantly exceeded supply.

Today Y-Fronts are the clear market leader in the branded underpant business with a 34% share of the market.

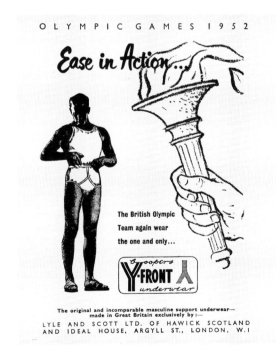

Bibliography

This list is not in any way fully inclusive of all books related to the companies contained within my book, but I hope it may lead some readers to find extra depths to companies I have had to cover in a more shallow way. Some have been supplied as reference points by the companies concerned, others I have since found in secondhand book shops and may not have been used by me for textual material.

The Firm of Cadbury 1831–1931
Iola A Williams (Constable 1931)

Clarks of Street 1925–1950
L H Barber (Clarks 1951)

A Furniture Maker
Lucian R Ercolani (Benn 1975)

The Endless Web:
John Dickinson & Co Ltd 1804–1954
Joan Evans (Jonathan Cape 1955)

Schweppes: The First 200 Years
Douglas A Simmons
(Springwood Books 1983)

Henry Tate 1819–1899
Tom Jones (Tate & Lyle Ltd 1960)

Pyrex: 60 Years of Design
(Tyne & Wear County Council
Museums 1983)

The Quaker Enterprise –
Friends in Business
David Burns Windsor
(Muller 1980)

Through the Mill
R G Burnett (Epworth 1945)

By Faith and Work:
Lord Mackintosh of Halifax
A A Thomson (Hutchinson 1966)

John Mackintosh - A Biography
G W Crutchley
(Hodder & Stoughton 1921)

Brooke Bond: A Hundred Years
David Wainwright
(Newman Neame)

C & J Clark 1825–1975
Brendan Lehane
(C & J Clark 1975)

The History of Bovril Advertising
Peter Hadley (Bovril Limited)

Fifty Years of Unilever 1930–1980
W J Reader (Heinemann 1980)

The Food Makers:
A History of General Foods Ltd
(General Foods 1972)

The Road from Aston Cross
Louise Wright
(Smedley–HP Foods Ltd 1975)

Wilsons of Guiseley 1877–1970
(Lawrence Wilson & Son Ltd)

100 Years of Progress
Nick Cutliffe
(H J Heinz Company Limited 1986)

The Story of Sunlight
Edmund Williams
(Unilever Plc 1984)

Port Sunlight:
The First Hundred Years
Edmund Williams
(Lever Brothers Limited 1988)

Addis 1780–1980:
All About the Home
Patrick Beaver
(Publications for Companies 1980)